Beginning Server-Side Application Development with Angular

Discover how to rapidly prototype SEO-friendly web applications with Angular Universal

Bram Borggreve

BIRMINGHAM - MUMBAI

Beginning Server-Side Application Development with Angular

First published: April 2018

Production reference: 1300418

Published by Packt Publishing Ltd.
Livery Place
35 Livery Street
Birmingham B3 2PB, UK.

ISBN 978-1-78934-216-1

www.packtpub.com

Credits

Author
Bram Borggreve

Reviewer
Juri Strumpflohner

Instructional Designer
Steven Fetterley

Acquisition Editor
Aditya Date

Development Editor
Taabish Khan

Production Coordinator
Vishal Pawar

Contributors

About the author

Bram Borggreve is a software engineer from The Netherlands, who currently works as a freelance developer and as an instructor at egghead.io. He is the founder of Colmena Consultancy LLC., a software development company specializing in designing and developing software solutions that are both modern and secure. With almost 20 years of experience in all fields of the software life cycle, Bram has a complete overview of the challenges that clients present him. Besides coding and mentoring, he likes traveling the world, meeting interesting people, and speaking multiple languages.

About the reviewer

Juri Strumpflohner is a software developer. He currently works as a software architect and frontend developer at R3-GIS, in beautiful South Tyrol (Italy). His main tasks are on the frontend, working with JavaScript, TypeScript, AngularJS, and Angular. He is also a Google developer expert in web technologies, an Egghead instructor, and happens to organize the Software Craftsmanship Meetup.

Packt is searching for authors like you

If you're interested in becoming an author for Packt, please visit `authors.packtpub.com` and apply today. We have worked with thousands of developers and tech professionals, just like you, to help them share their insight with the global tech community. You can make a general application, apply for a specific hot topic that we are recruiting an author for, or submit your own idea.

`mapt.io`

Mapt is an online digital library that gives you full access to over 5,000 books and videos, as well as industry leading tools to help you plan your personal development and advance your career. For more information, please visit our website.

Why subscribe?

- Spend less time learning and more time coding with practical eBooks and Videos from over 4,000 industry professionals
- Improve your learning with Skill Plans built especially for you
- Get a free eBook or video every month
- Mapt is fully searchable
- Copy and paste, print, and bookmark content

PacktPub.com

Did you know that Packt offers eBook versions of every book published, with PDF and ePub files available? You can upgrade to the eBook version at `www.PacktPub.com` and as a print book customer, you are entitled to a discount on the eBook copy. Get in touch with us at `service@packtpub.com` for more details.

At `www.PacktPub.com`, you can also read a collection of free technical articles, sign up for a range of free newsletters, and receive exclusive discounts and offers on Packt books and eBooks.

Table of Contents

Preface

Web applications built with Angular can be optimized for search engine optimization (SEO). Wikipedia defines SEO as "the process of affecting the online visibility of a website or a web page in a web search engine's unpaid results—often referred to as "natural", "organic", or "earned" results." Optimizing your app for search engines means your app is more visible on the internet and can drive more revenue for you or your client. Angular provides built-in features that can be leveraged to ensure our apps enjoy maximum visibility on the web.

In this book, you will learn how to use Angular to create a progressive web app (PWA) that has great support for SEO. This learning journey begins by identifying what makes an app SEO friendly and installing Angular CLI. You will then build out the UI components and the application components. By the end of the first lesson, you will have an app ready that is built using Angular's best practices. In the remaining two lessons, you will implement server-side rendering and service workers in your app. You will create the server app, implement an Express server, and add dynamic metadata to your app. Finally, you will configure service workers and test the offline capabilities of your app.

By the end of this book, you will be equipped to create modern, SEO-friendly web apps with best practices using Angular CLI.

What This Book Covers

Lesson 1, *Creating the Base Application*, shows how to install Angular CLI and create the Angular application that will be used in this book. We will set a few default settings and configure our global styles with Bootstrap and Font Awesome. We will then create the basic UI and layout of our app.

Lesson 2, *Creating the Application Module and Components*, explains the different types of components such as presentational components and container components. We will then see how to create PostsComponent, ProfileComponent, PostListComponent, PostItemComponent, and ProfileItemComponent. Finally, we will create resolvers to retrieve data using the router.

Lesson 3, *Server-Side Rendering*, shows how to add server-side rendering to our application. We will start by generating the server app and adding its dependencies. We will then add scripts to our package.json file, before implementing a web server in Express.js. Lastly, we will see how to add dynamic metadata to our pages.

Lesson 4, *Service Workers*, shows how to work with service workers. We will start by installing the required dependencies. We will then move on to enabling the service worker, configuring it, testing it, and finally debugging it.

What You Need for This Book

This book will require the following minimum hardware requirements:

- Processor: i3
- Memory: 2 GB RAM
- Hard disk: 10 GB
- Internet connection

Throughout this book, we will be using Node and npm to run our development environment, which is based on Angular CLI. Additionally, Git is needed in order to retrieve content from GitHub. Please ensure you have the following installed on your machine:

- Node 6.9.0 or higher
- npm 3.0 or higher
- Git

Checking the Version

We can check if our machine meets the requirements by checking the version of Node, npm, and Git. This can be done using the following commands:

```
node -v
npm -v
git --version
```

Development API

This book focuses on building an Angular application that functions as a public website. It will retrieve the content from a REST API to match real-life use cases as close as possible. The development API can be downloaded from GitHub and installed on local machines from

Installation of the API

To install the API, run the following commands:

```
$ git clone <repo_url>
$ cd packt-angular-seo-api
$ npm install
$ npm start
```

If all went well, you should see the following message in the terminal:

```
Web server listening at: http://localhost:3000
Browse your REST API at http://localhost:3000/explorer
```

Who This Book is for

This book is ideal for experienced front-end developers who are looking to quickly work through an intelligent example that demonstrates all the key features of server-side development with Angular. You'll need some prior exposure to Angular, as we skim over the basics and get straight to work.

You must also be well-versed with the following concepts:

- Basics of Angular
- HTML
- CSS
- Basics of TypeScript

Conventions

In this book, you will find a number of text styles that distinguish between different kinds of information. Here are some examples of these styles and an explanation of their meaning.

Code words and C++ language keywords *in text* are shown as follows: "We will update our `PostsComponent` to read the data that has been resolved by our router."

Folder names, filenames, file extensions, pathnames, include file names in text are shown as follows: "The header file `boost/asio.hpp` includes most of the types and functions required for using the Asio library".

A block of code is set as follows:

```
import { PostsResolver } from './resolvers/posts-resolver'

import { ProfileResolver } from './resolvers/profile-resolver'
```

New terms and important words are shown in bold. Words that you see on the screen, for example, in menus or dialog boxes, appear in the text like this: "If we check in the **Network** tab in Chrome Developer Tools, we see that we make two requests to the same endpoint."

Important new **programming terms** are shown in bold. *Conceptual terms* are shown in italics.

 Important additional details about a topic appear like this, as in a sidebar.

 Important notes, tips, and tricks appear like this.

Reader Feedback

Feedback from our readers is always welcome. Let us know what you think about this book—what you liked or disliked. Reader feedback is important for us as it helps us develop titles that you will really get the most out of.

To send us general feedback, simply e-mail feedback@packtpub.com, and mention the book's title in the subject of your message.

If there is a topic that you have expertise in and you are interested in either writing or contributing to a book, see our author guide at www.packtpub.com/authors.

Customer Support

Now that you are the proud owner of a Packt book, we have a number of things to help you to get the most from your purchase.

Downloading the Example Code

You can download the example code files from your account at http://www.packtpub.com for all the Packt Publishing books you have purchased. If you purchased this book elsewhere, you can visit http://www.packtpub.com/support and register to have the files e-mailed directly to you.

Errata

Although we have taken every care to ensure the accuracy of our content, mistakes do happen. If you find a mistake in one of our books—maybe a mistake in the text or the code—we would be grateful if you could report this to us. By doing so, you can save other readers from frustration and help us improve subsequent versions of this book. If you find any errata, please report them by visiting http://www.packtpub.com/submit-errata, selecting your book, clicking on the **Errata Submission Form** link, and entering the details of your errata. Once your errata are verified, your submission will be accepted and the errata will be uploaded to our website or added to any list of existing errata under the Errata section of that title.

To view the previously submitted errata, go to https://www.packtpub.com/books/content/support and enter the name of the book in the search field. The required information will appear under the **Errata** section.

Piracy

Piracy of copyrighted material on the Internet is an ongoing problem across all media. At Packt, we take the protection of our copyright and licenses very seriously. If you come across any illegal copies of our works in any form on the Internet, please provide us with the location address or website name immediately so that we can pursue a remedy.

Please contact us at `copyright@packtpub.com` with a link to the suspected pirated material.

We appreciate your help in protecting our authors and our ability to bring you valuable content.

Questions

If you have a problem with any aspect of this book, you can contact us at `questions@packtpub.com`, and we will do our best to address the problem.

1

Creating the Base Application

The Angular application we will build is a list of posts you regularly see in a social app such as Twitter. Each of these posts is posted by a user and we can click through to the user's profile to show all the posts made by the profile.

We will intentionally keep the application simple as the book is meant to focus on the technology rather than the functionality of the app. Although the app is simple, we will develop it using all the best practices of Angular development.

Web applications built with Angular can be optimized for search engines (SEO). Building support for SEO in apps means that search engines can read and understand the pages, and that the pages have dynamic data that is specifically aimed at search engines (meta tags). This increases the visibility of your app, giving higher search rankings and more links, resulting in more revenues for you or your client. Angular provides built-in features that can be leveraged to ensure apps enjoy maximum visibility on the web.

Lesson Objectives

In this lesson, you will:

- Install Angular CLI
- Create an Angular application
- Create the base UI of the application
- Create the header and footer of our application

Server-Side and Client-Side Rendering

When we talk about server-side rendering of websites, we are generally referring to an application or website that uses a programming language that runs on a server. On this server, the web pages are created (rendered) and the output of that rendering (the HTML) is sent to the browser, where it can be displayed directly.

 The code bundle for this book is hosted on GitHub at
https://github.com/TrainingByPackt/Beginning-Server-Side-Application-Development-with-Angular

When we talk about client-side rendering, we are generally referring to an application or website that uses JavaScript running in the browser to display (render) the pages. There is often a single page that is downloaded, with a JavaScript file that builds up the actual page (hence the term *single-page application*).

Installing Angular CLI

Angular CLI is the officially supported tool for creating and developing Angular applications. It is an open source project that is maintained by the Angular team and is the recommended way to develop Angular applications.

Angular CLI offers the following functionality:

- Create a new application
- Run the application in development mode
- Generate code using the best practices from the Angular team
- Run unit tests and end-to-end tests
- Create a production-ready build

One of the main benefits of using Angular CLI is that you don't need to configure any build tools. It's all abstracted away and available through one handy command: ng.

Throughout the book, we will be using the ng command for creating the app, generating the code, running the application in development mode, and creating builds.

 For more information about Angular CLI, refer to the project page on GitHub (`https://github.com/angular/angular-cli`)

To install Angular CLI on your machine, perform the following steps:

1. Open your terminal.
2. Run the following command:

    ```
    npm install -g @angular/cli@latest
    ```

3. Once the installation is finished without any errors, make sure that the ng command works as expected by running the following command:

    ```
    ng --version
    ```

4. Verify that the output is similar to the output shown here:

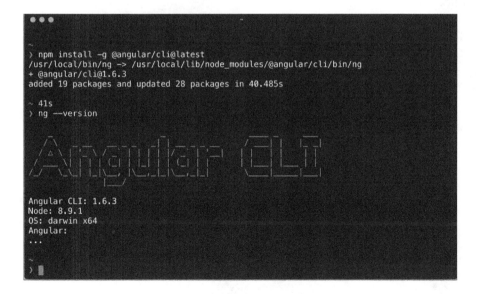

In this section, we have installed Angular CLI. We can start building our application!

Generating a New Application

Now that we have installed and configured Angular CLI, we can start generating our new application.

Running the `ng new` command will do the following:

- Create a folder called `angular-social`
- Create a new basic application inside this folder
- Add a routing module (because the `--routing` flag is passed in)
- Run `npm install` inside this folder to install the dependencies
- Run `git init` to initialize a new Git repository

Creating a New Application

To create a new application, perform the following steps:

1. Open your terminal and navigate to the directory where you want to work on your application:

   ```
   cd dev
   ```

2. Once inside your workspace directory, invoke the `ng` command as follows:

   ```
   ng new angular-social --routing
   ```

3. The output of this command will be similar to the following:

```
●●●                                      ~/dev
~/dev
› ng new angular-social --routing
  create angular-social/README.md (1029 bytes)
  create angular-social/.angular-cli.json (1249 bytes)
  create angular-social/.editorconfig (245 bytes)
  create angular-social/.gitignore (516 bytes)
  create angular-social/src/assets/.gitkeep (0 bytes)
  create angular-social/src/environments/environment.prod.ts (51 bytes)
  create angular-social/src/environments/environment.ts (387 bytes)
  create angular-social/src/favicon.ico (5430 bytes)
  create angular-social/src/index.html (300 bytes)
  create angular-social/src/main.ts (370 bytes)
  create angular-social/src/polyfills.ts (2405 bytes)
  create angular-social/src/styles.css (80 bytes)
  create angular-social/src/test.ts (1085 bytes)
  create angular-social/src/tsconfig.app.json (211 bytes)
  create angular-social/src/tsconfig.spec.json (304 bytes)
  create angular-social/src/typings.d.ts (104 bytes)
  create angular-social/e2e/app.e2e-spec.ts (296 bytes)
  create angular-social/e2e/app.po.ts (208 bytes)
  create angular-social/e2e/tsconfig.e2e.json (235 bytes)
  create angular-social/karma.conf.js (923 bytes)
  create angular-social/package.json (1326 bytes)
  create angular-social/protractor.conf.js (722 bytes)
  create angular-social/tsconfig.json (363 bytes)
  create angular-social/tslint.json (3040 bytes)
  create angular-social/src/app/app-routing.module.ts (245 bytes)
  create angular-social/src/app/app.module.ts (395 bytes)
  create angular-social/src/app/app.component.css (0 bytes)
  create angular-social/src/app/app.component.html (1173 bytes)
  create angular-social/src/app/app.component.spec.ts (1103 bytes)
  create angular-social/src/app/app.component.ts (207 bytes)
Installing packages for tooling via npm.
Successfully initialized git.
Project 'angular-social' successfully created.

~/dev 43s
›
```

Let's have a look at the folders that are created after running this command:

*   `src`: This folder contains the source files for our application

*   `src/app/`: This folder contains the application files

*   `src/assets/`: This folder contains the static assets we can use in our application (such as images)

*   `src/environments/`: This folder contains the definition of the default environments of our application

*   `e2e`: This folder contains the end-to-end tests for our application

Serving the Application

To serve the application, perform the following steps:

1. When the installation is finished, we can open our terminal and enter the working directory:

    ```
    cd angular-social
    ```

2. Run the `ng serve` command to start the development server:

    ```
    ng serve
    ```

    The output of the command will be as follows:

```
~/dev
> cd angular-social

~/dev/angular-social master
> ng serve
** NG Live Development Server is listening on localhost:4200, open your browser on http://localhost:
4200/ **
Date: 2018-01-11T11:48:20.737Z
Hash: b951f9869710a5db5a7f
Time: 6283ms
chunk {inline} inline.bundle.js (inline) 5.79 kB [entry] [rendered]
chunk {main} main.bundle.js (main) 22.4 kB [initial] [rendered]
chunk {polyfills} polyfills.bundle.js (polyfills) 552 kB [initial] [rendered]
chunk {styles} styles.bundle.js (styles) 33.8 kB [initial] [rendered]
chunk {vendor} vendor.bundle.js (vendor) 8.43 MB [initial] [rendered]

webpack: Compiled successfully.
```

Viewing Your Application

To view your application, perform the following steps:

1. Open your browser and navigate to `http://localhost:4200/`.

2. You should be greeted with a default page that says **Welcome to app!**:

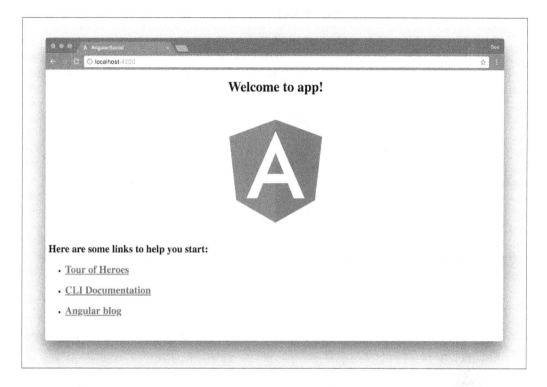

In this section, we have created a basic application using Angular CLI and viewed the same in the browser.

Setting Defaults for Angular CLI

Angular CLI works great out of the box and the default setup delivers a nice configuration to work with. But in addition to having some sane defaults, it is also very configurable.

In this book, we will take the opportunity to configure our Angular CLI defaults so it behaves a little bit differently.

The things we are going to change all have to do with how we generate (or scaffold) our code.

When scaffolding components, the default Angular CLI settings will create the HTML template and style sheet in a separate file.

In order to keep all component content in one file, we will configure Angular CLI to generate inline templates and styles.

The advantage of keeping all the component content in one file is that you can work on templates, styles, and the actual component code in a single place without having to switch files.

Configuring Global Defaults

In your terminal, run the following commands to globally configure the defaults:

```
ng set defaults.component.inlineStyle true
ng set defaults.component.inlineTemplate true
```

When we run the `git diff` command, we see that these settings are stored in the `.angular-cli.json` file in our application:

```
diff --git a/.angular-cli.json b/.angular-cli.json
index c6738d7..c0a8f24 100644
--- a/.angular-cli.json
+++ b/.angular-cli.json
@@ -55,6 +55,9 @@
     },
     "defaults": {
       "styleExt": "css",
-      "component": {}
+      "component": {
+        "inlineStyle": true,
+        "inlineTemplate": true
+      }
     }
   }
}
(END)
```

In this section, we have configured Angular CLI to generate inline styles and templates.

Configuring Global Styles

The default generated Angular application does not have any styling.

Angular does not dictate anything in terms of style, so in your own projects, you can use any other style framework, such as Angular Material, Foundation, Semantic UI, or one of the many others. Alternatively, you can create your own styles from scratch to get a unique look and feel.

For this book, though, we will stick to Bootstrap 4 and Font Awesome as they're widely used and they provide a great style with a minimal amount of added code.

Linking to the Style Sheets in global styles.css

As discussed in the previous section, our application comes with a global style sheet, `src/styles.css`.

In this style sheet, we will use the `@import` command to link to Bootstrap and Font Awesome. This will instruct Angular to download the files and apply the style to your application globally.

Adding Bootstrap and Font Awesome

1. Open the `src/styles.css` file in your editor.
2. Add the following two lines at the end of the file:
    ```
    @import url('https://maxcdn.bootstrapcdn.com/bootstrap/4.0.0-beta.2/css/
    bootstrap.min.css');
    @import url('https://maxcdn.bootstrapcdn.com/font-awesome/4.7.0/css/
    font-awesome.min.css');
    ```
3. Refresh the app in the browser.

As you can see, the font of the application was updated to a sans-serif font as that's the Bootstrap default:

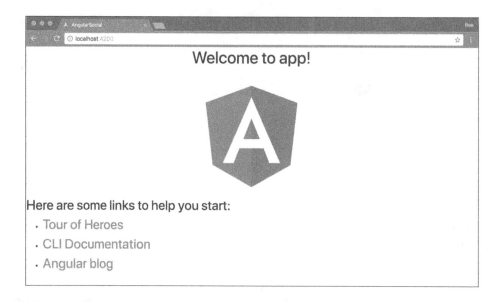

Showing an Icon on the Page

1. Open the `src/app.component.html` file and replace the content with the following:

```
<h1 class="text-center mt-5">
  <i class="fa fa-thumbs-up"></i>
</h1>
```

When the app refreshes in your browser, you should see the thumbs up icon in the center of the page:

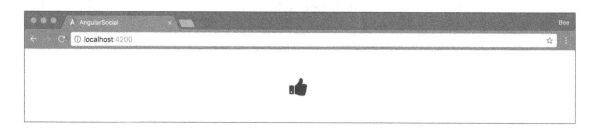

For a list of all available icons, you can refer to the *Font Awesome Cheatsheet* (http://fontawesome.io/cheatsheet/).

For an overview of all available Bootstrap styles, you can refer to the Bootstrap 4 documentation (https://getbootstrap.com/docs/4.0/getting-started/introduction/).

In this section, we have set up Bootstrap and Font Awesome as the style frameworks for our app. This will enable us to have a different font style than what Angular CLI provides. We can now start creating our UI components.

Creating UI Modules and Components

One of the great things about working with Angular is that it promotes building your applications in a modular and componentized way.

In Angular, an `NgModule` (or simply `Module`) is a way to group your application into logical blocks of functionality.

A `Module` is a TypeScript class with the `@NgModule` decorator. In the decorator, we define how Angular compiles and runs the code inside the module.

In this lesson, we are going to build a module that groups together all the components we want to use in our user interface.

We will add a `LayoutComponent` that consists of our `HeaderComponent` and `FooterComponent`, and in-between those, we will define the space where our application code will be displayed using the `RouterOutlet` component:

Creating the UiModule

In this section, we will generate the `UiModule` using the `ng` command and import the `UiModule` in the `AppModule`.

Using the `ng generate` command, we can generate or scaffold out all sorts of code that can be used in our Angular application.

We will use the `ng generate module` command to generate our `UiModule`.

This command has one required parameter, which is the name. In our application, we will call this module `ui`:

1. Open your terminal and navigate to the project directory.
2. Run the following command from inside the project directory:

```
$ ng generate module ui
    create src/app/ui/ui.module.ts (186 bytes)
```

As you can see from the output of the command, our `UiModule` is generated in the new folder `src/app/ui`:

```
~/dev/angular-social master
) ng generate module ui
   create src/app/ui/ui.module.ts (186 bytes)

~/dev/angular-social master*
) cat src/app/ui/ui.module.ts
import { NgModule } from '@angular/core';
import { CommonModule } from '@angular/common';

@NgModule({
  imports: [
    CommonModule
  ],
  declarations: []
})
export class UiModule { }

~/dev/angular-social master*
)
```

When we take a look at this file, we can see what an empty Angular module looks like:

```
import { NgModule } from '@angular/core';
import { CommonModule } from '@angular/common';

@NgModule({
  imports: [
    CommonModule
  ],
  declarations: []
})
export class UiModule { }
```

Importing Our UiModule

Now that our UiModule is created, we need to import it from our AppModule. That way, we can use the code inside the UiModule from other code that lives inside the AppModule:

1. Open the project in your editor.

2. Open the src/app/app.module.ts file.

3. Add the import statement on top of the file:

```
import { UiModule } from './ui/ui.module'
```

4. Add a reference to UiModule in the imports array inside the NgModule decorator:

```
@NgModule({
  ...
  imports: [
    // other imports
    UiModule
  ],
  ...
})
```

Our `UiModule` is now created and imported in our `AppModule`, which makes it ready to use.

Let's go ahead and create our first component inside the `UiModule`, and make it display in our app!

Displaying the Current Route

When building our app, we will heavily lean on Angular's router to tie all of our modules and components together.

Because we will build all the functionality in modules, we will use our main `AppComponent` only to display the current route. To make this work, we will need to update the `AppComponent` template and make sure we define the `router-outlet`:

1. Open the project in your editor.
2. Open the `src/app/app.component.html` file.
3. Remove all of the content and add the following HTML:

   ```
   <router-outlet></router-outlet>
   ```

After refreshing the app in our browser, we should see a blank page. This is because we don't have any routes set up and thus there is no way the Angular app knows what to display. Let's move to the next section to create our basic layout!

Creating the LayoutComponent

In this section, we will use `ng generate` to create the `LayoutComponent` inside the `UiModule` and add the `LayoutComponent` to the `AppRoutingModule` so it gets displayed.

The `LayoutComponent` is the main template of our application. Its function is to glue together the `HeaderComponent` and the `FooterComponent` and show the actual application pages in-between those two.

Now we will be using the `ng generate` command to create our `LayoutComponent`.

1. Open your terminal and navigate to the project directory.
2. Run the following command from inside the project directory:

    ```
    ng generate component ui/components/layout
    ```

When we look at the output, we see that our component was created in the new `src/app/ui/components` directory:

```
                                   ~/dev/angular-social
~/dev/angular-social master
> ng generate component ui/components/layout
  create src/app/ui/components/layout/layout.component.spec.ts (628 bytes)
  create src/app/ui/components/layout/layout.component.ts (256 bytes)
  update src/app/ui/ui.module.ts (273 bytes)

~/dev/angular-social master*
>
```

The last line of our output shows us that our `UiModule` was updated.

When we open our `UiModule` in our editor, we see that it added an `import` for our `LayoutComponent` and added it to the `declarations` array in the `NgModule` decorator.

The `declarations` array *declares* the existence of components in a module so Angular knows that they exist and can be used:

```
import { NgModule } from '@angular/core';
import { CommonModule } from '@angular/common';

@NgModule({
  imports: [
    CommonModule
```

```
  ],
  declarations: []
})
export class UiModule { }
```

Adding a New Route

As described earlier in this section, we will use our LayoutComponent as the base for the whole application. It will display our header, footer, and an outlet to show our actual application screens.

We will leverage Angular's built-in routing mechanism to do this. We will do this by adding a new route to the routing array, and reference the LayoutComponent in this route's component:

1. Open the src/app/app-routing.module.ts file.

2. Add an import to the list of imports on the top of the file:

   ```
   import { LayoutComponent } from './ui/components/layout/layout.
   component'
   ```

3. Inside the empty array that is assigned to the routes property, we add a new object literal.

4. Add the path property and set its value to an empty string ''.

5. Add the component property and set its value to the reference LayoutComponent that we just imported. The line of code that we add to our routes array is as follows:

   ```
   { path: '', component: LayoutComponent, children: [] },
   ```

For reference, the complete file should look like this:

```
import { NgModule } from '@angular/core';
import { Routes, RouterModule } from '@angular/router';
import { LayoutComponent } from './ui/components/layout/layout.component'

const routes: Routes = [
  { path: '', component: LayoutComponent, children: [] },
];

@NgModule({
  imports: [RouterModule.forRoot(routes)],
  exports: [RouterModule]
```

```
})
export class AppRoutingModule { }
```

When our application refreshes, we should see the text **layout works!**:

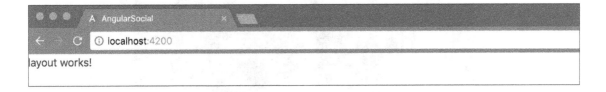

Building Our Layout

Let's get rid of this default text and start building our actual layout:

1. Open the `src/app/ui/layout/layout.component.ts` file.

2. Get rid of the contents of the `template` property.

3. Add the following contents to the empty `template` string:
   ```
   app-header placeholder
   <div class="container my-5">
       <router-outlet></router-outlet>
   </div>
   app-footer placeholder
   ```

When we save our file, we see that our browser outputs a blank page.

Looking in the **Console** tab from Chrome Developer Tools, we see that we have an error stating **Template parse errors: 'router-outlet' is not a known element**:

In order to make Angular aware of how to render the `router-outlet`, we need to import the `RouterModule`:

1. Open the `src/app/ui/ui.module.ts` file.

2. Add an `import` statement to the list of imports on the top of the file:

   ```
   import { RouterModule } from '@angular/router';
   ```

3. Add a reference to the `RouterModule` inside the `imports` array in the `NgModule` decorator.

```
import { NgModule } from '@angular/core';
import { CommonModule } from '@angular/common';
import { RouterModule } from '@angular/router';
import { LayoutComponent } from './components/layout/layout.component';

@NgModule({
  imports: [
    CommonModule,
    RouterModule,
  ],
  declarations: [LayoutComponent]
})
export class UiModule { }
```

When we now save the file, we should see the placeholders for our header and footer, with some white space in-between and the router error is now gone from our console:

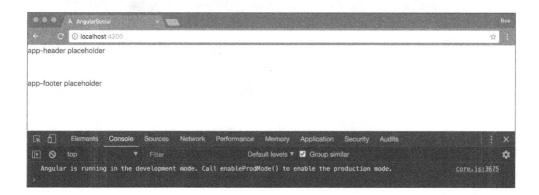

Now that that's done, let's add some content to the placeholders!

Creating the HeaderComponent

In this section, we will use ng generate to create the HeaderComponent inside the UiModule, reference the HeaderComponent from our LayoutComponent so it gets displayed, and implement the navigation bar with a dynamic title and items.

We will be using the ng generate command to create our HeaderComponent:

1. Open your terminal and navigate to the project directory.
2. Run the following command from inside the project directory:

```
ng g c ui/components/header
```

When we look at the output, we see that our component was created in the new src/app/ui/header directory and that our UiModule was updated, just as we would expect after having done the same for our LayoutComponent:

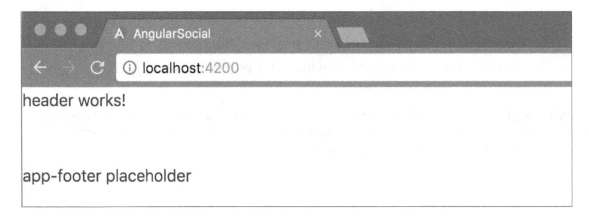

```
~/dev/angular-social master
) ng g c ui/components/header
  create src/app/ui/components/header/header.component.spec.ts (628 bytes)
  create src/app/ui/components/header/header.component.ts (256 bytes)
  update src/app/ui/ui.module.ts (430 bytes)

~/dev/angular-social master*
)
```

Updating the LayoutComponent to Reference Our New HeaderComponent

Now, we will update the `LayoutComponent` so that it references our new `HeaderComponent` instead of our `app-header` placeholder:

1. Open the `src/app/ui/components/layout/layout.component.ts` file.
2. Find the `app-header` placeholder and replace it with the following tag:

   `<app-header></app-header>`

When we see our application refresh in our browser, we see that we now have the string **header works!** instead of the placeholder:

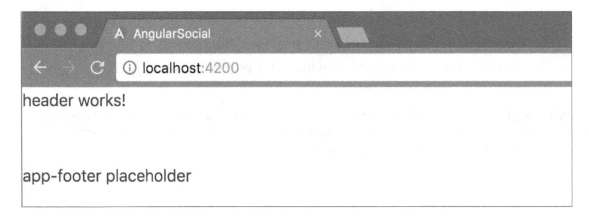

We can now start implementing our actual header so that our pages finally start to look like an app!

Creating the Actual Header

Now we will create the actual header. We will define three class properties, a string property for the application logo and title, and an array of objects that represent the links we want to display in our header.

In the template, we will create a Bootstrap navbar consisting of a `nav` element with some styles, a link with our logo and title, and the actual navigation links.

 More information on how to use the navbar can be found here: `https://getbootstrap.com/docs/4.0/components/navbar/`

1. Download the file from
   `https://angular.io/assets/images/logos/angular/angular.svg` and store it as `src/assets/logo.svg`.

2. Open the `src/app/ui/components/header/header.component.ts` file.

3. Inside the `component` class, we add three new properties:

```
public logo = 'assets/logo.svg';
public title = 'Angular Social';
public items = [{ label: 'Posts', url: '/posts'}];
```

4. Replace the contents of the `template` property with the following markup:

```
<nav class="navbar navbar-expand navbar-dark bg-dark">
   <a class="navbar-brand" routerLink="/">
     <img [src]="logo" width="30" height="30" alt="">

   </a>
   <div class="collapse navbar-collapse">
     <ul class="navbar-nav">
       <li class="nav-item" *ngFor="let item of items"
routerLinkActive="active">
         <a class="nav-link" [routerLink]="item.url">{{item.label}}</a>
       </li>
     </ul>
   </div>
</nav>
```

When we save this file and check in our browser, we finally see the first real part of the application being displayed. Things will move quickly from now on:

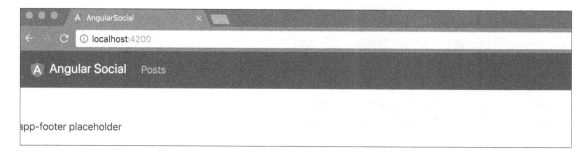

Let's apply the knowledge we have gained in this section to build the FooterComponent.

Creating the FooterComponent

In this section, we will use ng generate to create the FooterComponent inside the UiModule, reference the FooterComponent from our LayoutComponent so it gets displayed, and implement the footer and add a small copyright message.

We will be using the ng generate command to create our FooterComponent:

1. Open your terminal and navigate to the project directory.
2. Run the following command from inside the project directory:

```
$ ng g c ui/components/footer
```

When we look at the output, we see that our component got created in the new src/app/ui/footer directory and that our UiModule was updated, similar to what happened in the previous sections:

```
~/dev/angular-social                                    ~/dev/angular-social
~/dev/angular-social master
) ng g c ui/components/footer
  create src/app/ui/components/footer/footer.component.spec.ts (628 bytes)
  create src/app/ui/components/footer/footer.component.ts (256 bytes)
  update src/app/ui/ui.module.ts (519 bytes)

~/dev/angular-social master*
) █
```

Updating the LayoutComponent to Reference Our New FooterComponent

We will update the `LayoutComponent` so that it references our new `FooterComponent` instead of our `app-footer` placeholder:

1. Open the `src/app/ui/components/layout/layout.component.ts` file.
2. Find the `app-footer` placeholder and replace it with the following tag:

    ```
    <app-footer></app-footer>
    ```

Just like with our header, we see after refreshing our application that we now have the string **footer works!** instead of the placeholder:

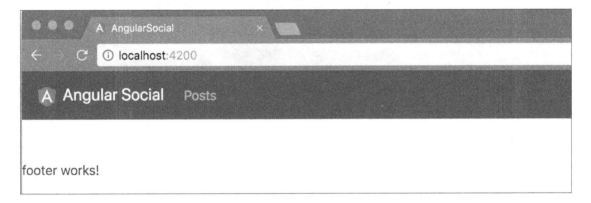

The last step is to implement the footer and our base layout is done!

Creating the Actual Footer

Now we will create the actual footer. We will define two class properties, a string property for the name of the developer, and the year.

In the template, we will create another Bootstrap navbar consisting of a `nav` element with some styles and the copyright message that uses both string properties we defined in our component class:

1. Open the `src/app/ui/components/footer/footer.component.ts` file.
2. Inside the `component` class, add the following property. Don't forget to update the two placeholders with the right data:

    ```
    public developer = 'YOUR_NAME_PLACEHOLDER';
    ```

```
public year = 'YEAR_PLACEHOLDER';
```

3. Get rid of the contents of the `template` property.

4. Replace the contents of the `template` property with the following markup:

```
<nav class="navbar fixed-bottom navbar-expand navbar-dark bg-dark">
    <div class="navbar-text m-auto">
        {{developer}} <i class="fa fa-copyright"></i> {{year}}
    </div>
</nav>
```

When we save this file and check in our browser, we finally see that the footer is being rendered:

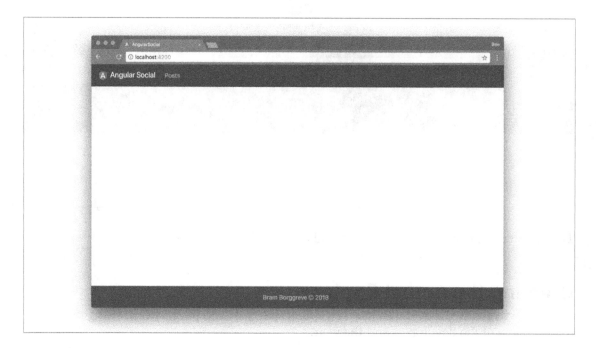

We are done with our layout! In this section, we've built our header and footer components. We've also built our layout component and created a `UiModule`. Let's get to building our actual application logic.

Summary

In this lesson, we installed Angular CLI and created the Angular application. We set a few default settings and configured our global styles with Bootstrap and Font Awesome. We then created the basic UI and layout of our app. Finally, we implemented a header and a footer in our app.

In the next lesson, we will create the application module and components.

2

Creating the Application Module and Components

In this lesson, we will start by creating a `PostsModule` that contains all the code related to displaying the posts that come from our API.

Inside this module, we will add various components, a service, and two resolvers.

The components are used to display the data in the browser. We will go over their use in this lesson. The service is used to retrieve the data from the API. Lastly, we will add resolvers to our app; resolvers make sure the data from the service is available at the moment we navigate from one route to another.

Lesson Objectives

- Explore the types of components that will be used in our app
- Create and load the PostsModule
- Create the container components, such as PostsComponent and ProfileComponent
- Add dummy posts and profiles
- Create a service to retrieve data
- Create the presentational components, such as PostListComponent, PostItemComponent, and ProfileItemComponent
- Create and import resolvers

Types of Components

In this section, we will take a look at how we can differentiate our components by making a distinction between **container** and **presentational** components. Sometimes, they are also called *smart* and *dumb* components, referring to how much *knowledge* of the world outside of the components each of them has.

The main difference we can make is the following:

- A presentational component is responsible for *how things look*
- A container component is responsible for *how things work*

We will dive into more details of why this distinction is important when we create them, but we can give away a few things already.

Presentational Components

We can say the following about presentational components:

- They get their data *passed in* using the @Input() decorator
- Any operations are *passed up* using the @Output() decorator
- They handle the markup and the styling of the application
- They mostly just contain other presentational components
- They have no knowledge (or dependencies) on any routes or services from the app

Container Components

We can say the following about container components:

- They retrieve their data from a service or a resolver
- They handle the operations that they receive from the presentational components
- They have very little markup and styling
- They will often contain both presentational and container components

Folder Structure

To make the distinction clear in our project, we will use different folders for each type of component:

- The `src/<module>/components` folder is where the presentational components live
- The `src/<module>/containers` folder is where the container components live

Generate and Lazy Load the PostsModule

We will generate the `PostsModule` using the `ng` command and lazy load the `PostsModule` in the `AppRoutingModule`.

Using the `ng generate` command, we can generate or scaffold out all sorts of code that can be used in our Angular application.

We will use the `ng generate module` command to generate our `PostsModule`.

This command has one required parameter, which is the name. In our application, we will call this module `posts`. A second optional parameter is passed in in order to create a separate file to hold the routes for this module, the `PostsRoutingModule`:

1. Open your terminal and navigate to the project directory.
2. Run the following command from inside the project directory:

   ```
   ng g m posts --routing
   ```

As you can see from the output of the command, our `PostsModule` is generated in the new folder `src/app/posts`:

```
~/dev/angular-social master 8s
> ng g m posts --routing
  create src/app/posts/posts-routing.module.ts (248 bytes)
  create src/app/posts/posts.module.ts (275 bytes)

~/dev/angular-social master*
>
```

In contrast to how we load our `UiModule` by importing it into our `AppModule`, we will lazy load our `PostsModule` using our `AppRoutingModule`.

This is an optimization of how our application is built and it makes sure that our application has a smaller initial file to download by using a technology called **code splitting**. This basically bundles each lazy loaded module into its own file and the browser is instructed to download this file when needed, but not before.

We will add two routes to our main application file. The first route is a route with a blank `path` property (our default route) and its function is to redirect to the `/posts` route.

The second route is the `/posts` route and it lazy loads the `PostsModule`.

If the user navigates to the app, the first route that will be found is our blank redirect route. This will tell the router to navigate to `/posts`. The router finds the `/posts` route and navigates the user to that module:

1. Open the project in your editor.
2. Open the `src/app/app-routing.module.ts` file.
3. Locate our only existing route object that is defined in the `routes` property.
4. Inside this new `children` array, we create two routes that look like this:

    ```
    { path: '', redirectTo: '/posts', pathMatch: 'full'},
    { path: 'posts', loadChildren: './posts/posts.module#PostsModule' },
    ```

    Make sure that the complete `routes` property looks like this:

    ```
    const routes: Routes = [
      { path: '', component: LayoutComponent, children: [
        { path: '', redirectTo: '/posts', pathMatch: 'full'},
        { path: 'posts', loadChildren: './posts/posts.module#PostsModule' },
      ] },
    ];
    ```

Here are a few things to explain how this works:

*   First, we define that we want to have children to our main route. This makes sure that all of our children get rendered in the `<router-outlet>` that is defined in the `LayoutComponent` in the *Creating the LayoutComponent* section.
*   We define our first route to respond to all paths (that's what the empty string does), and we tell it to redirect to the `/posts` route.
*   Lastly, we create a `posts` route and we tell it to load its children from our new module. The `loadChildren` property is what enables the lazy loading.

When we refresh our page in the browser, we can see that nothing changes in the app itself, but we can see that our URL has changed; it has redirected to /posts.

Let's move on to the next section to create our container components so that we can start seeing data!

Creating the Container Components

In this section, we will use ng generate to create the PostsComponent and ProfileComponent inside the PostsModule, add routes to both components, and add dummy data that we can use to build our presentational components.

Creating PostsComponent and ProfileComponent

We will be using the ng generate command to create our PostsComponent. This is the component that will eventually list an overview for all our posts.

The application route to this component will be /posts:

1. Open your terminal and navigate to the project directory.
2. Run the following command from inside the project directory:

   ng g c posts/containers/posts

   ```
   ~/dev/angular-social
   ~/dev/angular-social master
   > ng g c posts/containers/posts
     create src/app/posts/containers/posts/posts.component.spec.ts (621 bytes)
     create src/app/posts/containers/posts/posts.component.ts (253 bytes)
     update src/app/posts/posts.module.ts (358 bytes)
   ~/dev/angular-social master*
   >
   ```

3. Open the src/app/posts/posts-routing.module.ts file.
4. Import the PostsComponent:

   import { PostsComponent } from './containers/posts/posts.component'

5. Add the following route to the routes array:

```
{ path: '', component: PostsComponent },
```

Now when we refresh the page in our app, we should see the text **posts works!** between our header and footer:

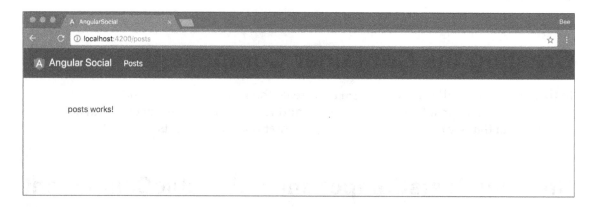

Very similar to how we created the PostsComponent, we will now create the ProfileComponent. This is the component that will be responsible for displaying the profile that made the post.

The application route to this component will be /posts/<id>, where <id> is the identifier of the profile we want to display:

1. Open your terminal and navigate to the project directory.

2. Run the following command from inside the project directory:

```
ng g c posts/containers/profile
```

```
~/dev/angular-social master*
> ng g c posts/containers/profile
  create src/app/posts/containers/profile/profile.component.spec.ts (635 bytes)
  create src/app/posts/containers/profile/profile.component.ts (259 bytes)
  update src/app/posts/posts.module.ts (451 bytes)

~/dev/angular-social master*
>
```

3. Open the src/app/posts/posts-routing.module.ts file.

4. Import the `ProfileComponent`:

```
import { ProfileComponent } from './containers/profile/profile.
component'
```

5. Add the following route to the `routes` array:

```
{ path: ':profileId', component: ProfileComponent },
```

When our application refreshes and we navigate our browser to `http://localhost:4200/posts/1`, we should see the text **profile works!**:

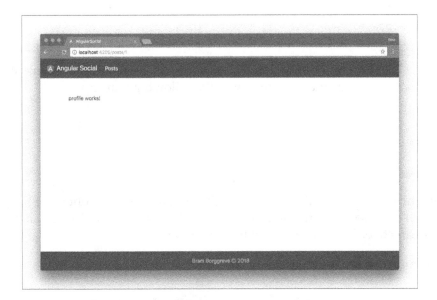

Adding Dummy Post and Profile Data

In order to get a feel of how our application works, we will add some dummy data to our components so we have something to work with. We will add a service to retrieve the data from our API:

1. Open the `src/app/posts/containers/posts/posts.component.ts` file.

2. Create a new property called `posts` and define it with the following structure:

```
public posts = []
```

3. Add the following `import` to the top of the file:

```
import { ActivatedRoute } from '@angular/router';
```

4. The `items` array inside our `posts` object is what will eventually hold our posts. We will use a simple loop to add a few dummy items.

5. Locate the `ngOnInit()` method and add the following code to the method body. This code creates 10 dummy elements in our `posts` array so we can display some data. The details are not relevant as this block will be obsolete in the next lesson when we retrieve data from our API:

```
for(let i = 1; i < 10; i++) {
    this.posts.push({ id: i, text: 'This is post with id: ' + i })
 }
```

6. For the last step, we need to update our template. Remove all the content from the `template` property and replace it with the following markup:

```
<div *ngFor="let post of posts">
    <a [routerLink]="post.id">
      {{post.text}}
    </a>
</div>
```

The code in our template uses the `ngFor` directive to loop over the content of the `posts` array. For each of those items, it prints an `a` tag that links to the post by `id` using the `routerLink` directive. The link text is set to `post.text`.

This is what we get in the browser:

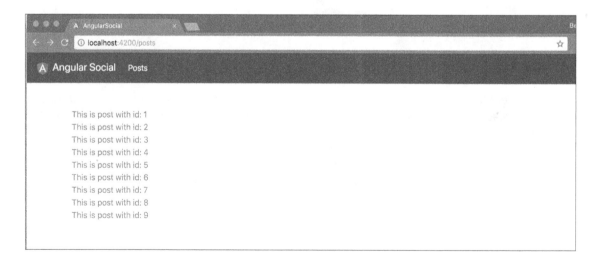

Lastly, we will add some dummy data to our `ProfileComponent`:

1. Open the `src/app/posts/containers/profile/profile.component.ts` file.

2. Create a new property called `profile` and define it with the following structure:

```
public profile = { id: null };
```

3. Add the following `import` to the top of the file:

```
import { ActivatedRoute } from '@angular/router';
```

4. Locate the `constructor()` method and add the following code to the method parameters:

```
constructor(private route:ActivatedRoute){}
```

5. Locate the `ngOnInit()` method and add the following code to the method body. This code *subscribes* to the parameters of the current route and when it changes, it reads the value of the `profileId` property in the URL and assigns it to the `id` property of `this.profile`:

```
this.route.params.subscribe(res => this.profile.id = 'profileId = ' +
res['profileId'])
```

6. For the last step, we need to update our template. Remove all the content from the `template` property and replace it with the following markup:

```
<p>
  {{profile.id}}
</p>
```

When we go to `http://localhost:4200/posts/5`, we will see the following:

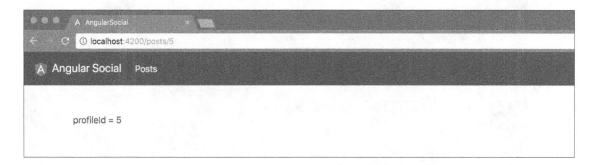

The code in the `ngOnInit` block *subscribes* to the parameters of the *activated route*. When we retrieve that on that subscription, we use it to append the ID to the string in the `post.text` property, making the content dynamic.

We can now click through from the `PostsContainer` to the `ProfileContainer` component. We can use the Back button or the link in the header to go back.

Our container components are set up and the routes work. Let's add some real data from the API!

Creating a Service to Retrieve Data

In this section, we will use `ng generate` to create the `PostsService`, use `environment` to store the API URL, and use the `PostsService` in our components. We will then define our API calls in the `PostsService` and leverage the `HttpClientModule` to enable HTTP access.

Generating the Service

We will use the `ng generate service` command to generate a service that will handle the interaction with our API:

1. Open your terminal and navigate to the project directory.
2. Run the following command from inside the project directory:

```
ng g s posts/services/posts --module posts/posts
```

```
                                                    ~/dev/angular-social
~/dev/angular-social master
> ng g s posts/services/posts --module posts/posts
  create src/app/posts/services/posts.service.spec.ts (368 bytes)
  create src/app/posts/services/posts.service.ts (111 bytes)
  update src/app/posts/posts.module.ts (537 bytes)

~/dev/angular-social master*
>
```

Storing Our API URL

We will use the `environment` of Angular CLI to store our API URL. Using the `environment`, we can define a different URL for development and production environments.

By default, the application generated with Angular CLI comes with two predefined environments. These environments are defined in `.angular-cli.json` in the project root.

1. Open the `src/environments/environment.ts` file.

2. Inside the `environment` variable, add an `apiUrl` key and assign as the value the string `http://localhost:3000/api`, which is the URL to the development API:

3. Open the `src/environments/environment.prod.ts` file.

4. Inside the `environment` variable, add an `apiUrl` key and assign as the value the string `https://packt-angular-social.now.sh/api`, which is the URL to the production API:

Referencing Our New PostsService in Our Container Components

In this service, we will reference our new `PostsService` in our container components and that way define what our service should look like.

We will use the `OnInit` component life cycle hook provided by Angular to call into our inject service and invoke the `getPosts` method on that service.

We will *map* over the result to only get the items and then we will subscribe and set the result of the method to our `posts` property.

Note that we do the same thing for both the `PostsComponent` and the `ProfileComponent`:

1. Open the `src/app/posts/containers/posts/posts.component.ts` file.

2. Add an `import` statement for our new `PostsService`:

    ```
    import { PostsService } from '../../services/posts.service';
    ```

3. Update the constructor to *inject* the `PostsService` and make it available under the `private postsService` variable:

    ```
    constructor(private postsService: PostsService) { }
    ```

4. Remove the contents of the `ngOnInit` method and update it as follows:

```
ngOnInit() {
  this.postsService.getPosts()
    .map(res => res['items'])
    .subscribe((result: any) => this.posts = result)
}
```

5. Open the `src/app/posts/containers/posts/profile.component.ts` file.

6. Add an `import` statement for our new `PostsService`:

```
import { PostsService } from '../services/posts.service';
```

7. Update the constructor to *inject* the `PostsService`, and make sure to leave our `private route` dependency in place:

```
constructor(private route: ActivatedRoute, private postsService:
PostsService) { }
```

8. Remove the contents of the `ngOnInit` method and update it as follows:

```
this.postsService.getProfile(this.route.snapshot.params['profileId'])
  .subscribe((result: any) => this.profile = result)
```

Defining the Public Methods

The next step is to define our public methods in our `PostsService` and make sure that these retrieve the data we need from our API.

We will add two methods in our `PostsService`. The first method is the `getPosts` method, which does not take any arguments and returns all the posts from the API. The second method is the `getProfile` method, which takes the `profileId` as an argument. It returns the profile related to the `profileId` that is passed in as the argument, and includes all the related posts that are made by that profile:

1. Open the `src/app/posts/services/posts.service.ts` file.

2. Add an `import` statement to import the `HttpClient` from `@angular/common/http` and a reference to the `environment` where we have our API URL defined:

```
import { HttpClient } from '@angular/common/http';
import { environment } from '../../../environments/environment'
```

3. Update the constructor to inject the `HttpClient` and make it available under the `private http` variable:

```
constructor(private http: HttpClient) { }
```

4. Create a new method called `getPosts()  {}` and add the following content:

```
getPosts() {
    const url = `${environment.apiUrl}/posts/timeline?filter[where]
[type]=text`
    return this.http.get(url)
}
```

5. Create a new method called `getProfile(profileId)  {  }` and add the following content:

```
getProfile(profileId) {
    const url = `${environment.apiUrl}/profiles/${profileId}?filter[inclu
de]=posts`
    return this.http.get(url)
}
```

Importing HttpClientModule in Our AppModule

We are almost done creating our `PostsService`, but there is still one thing we need to fix. When we refresh our application in our browser, we see that we have an error message in our **Console** tab:

The reason we get this error is because we have used the `HttpClient` in our service, but Angular does not know where this module comes from. In order to fix this, we need to import `HttpClientModule` in our `AppModule`:

1. Open the `src/app/app.module.ts` file.

2. Add an `import` statement to import the `HttpClientModule` from `@angular/common/http`:

   ```
   import { HttpClientModule } from '@angular/common/http';
   ```

3. Update the `imports` array in the `NgModule` decorator to import `HttpClientModule`:

   ```
   @NgModule({
       ...
       imports: [
           ...
         HttpClientModule,
           ...
       ],
       ...
   })
   ```

When we now check the **Console** tab, we see that there is another error message, **.map is not a function**:

To fix this, we need to import the map operator from the rxjs library.

The rxjs library is one of the main dependencies of Angular and is used to implement the *Observable* pattern in Angular. It is used by Angular itself in the router and the HTTP client.

The map operator is one of the operators shipped by rxjs and it can be used to map over the data before you subscribe to it. This is useful if you want to manipulate the data you work with:

1. Open the src/app/app.module.ts file.

2. Add an import statement to import the map operator from the rxjs library:

   ```
   import 'rxjs/add/operator/map';
   ```

When we now refresh our application, we should see a list of posts retrieved from the API!

Let's continue to add some presentational components to give our posts some style!

Creating the Presentational Components

In this section, we will use `ng generate component` to create the `PostListComponent` and `PostItemComponent` inside the `PostsModule`. We will then add a UI to these components and use these components in our container components.

The `PostListComponent` is responsible for taking in an array of posts using its *Input*, and it loops over each of these posts and invokes the `PostItemComponent`.

The `PostItemComponent` accepts a single post as its *Input* and displays that post.

Creating the PostListComponent

We will be using the `ng generate` command to create our `PostListComponent`. This is the component that will loop over our posts and will be called from our `PostsComponent`:

1. Open the `src/app/posts/container/posts/posts.component.ts` file.
2. Update the template to the following:

   ```
   <app-post-list [posts]="posts"></app-post-list>
   ```

3. Open your terminal and navigate to the project directory.
4. Run the following command from inside the project directory:

   ```
   ng g c posts/components/post-list
   ```

```
~/dev/angular-social master
> ng g c posts/components/post-list
  create src/app/posts/components/post-list/post-list.component.spec.ts (643 bytes)
  create src/app/posts/components/post-list/post-list.component.ts (264 bytes)
  update src/app/posts/posts.module.ts (636 bytes)

~/dev/angular-social master*
>
```

5. Open the `src/app/posts/components/post-list/post-list.component.ts` file.

6. Import the `Input` from `@angular/core` by adding it to the existing `import` statement.

7. Add the following property in the component class:

   ```
   @Input() posts: any[]
   ```

8. Update the template to the following:

   ```
   <div *ngFor="let post of posts" class="mb-3">
     <app-post-item [post]="post"></app-post-item>
   </div>
   ```

Creating the PostItemComponent

We will be using the `ng generate` command to create our `PostItemComponent`:

1. Open your terminal and navigate to the project directory.

2. Run the following command from inside the project directory:

   ```
   ng g c posts/components/post-item
   ```

```
~/dev/angular-social master*
> ng g c posts/components/post-item
  create src/app/posts/components/post-item/post-item.component.spec.ts (643 bytes)
  create src/app/posts/components/post-item/post-item.component.ts (264 bytes)
  update src/app/posts/posts.module.ts (735 bytes)

~/dev/angular-social master*
>
```

3. Open the `src/app/posts/components/post-item/post-item.component.ts` file.

4. Import the `Input` from `@angular/core` by adding it to the existing `import` statement.

5. Add the following property in the component class:

```
@Input() post: any;
```

6. Update the template to the following:

```
<!-- The row and the col make sure the content is always centered -->
<div class="row">
  <div class="col-md-8 offset-md-2">
    <!-- The card is where the message is shown -->
    <div class="card">
      <div class="card-body">
        <!-- We use the Bootstrap 'media' component to show an avatar
with content -->
        <div class="media">
          <img class="avatar mr-3 rounded" [attr.src]="post?.profile?.
avatar">
          <div class="media-body">
            <!-- The full name of the author is used to navigate to the
post detail -->
            <h5>
              <a [routerLink]="post?.profile?.id"> {{post?.profile?.
fullName}} </a>
              <span class="date float-right text-muted">

              </span>
            </h5>
            <!-- The text of the post is shown in a simple paragraph
tag-->
            <p>{{post?.text}}</p>
          </div>
        </div> <!-- End media -->
      </div>
    </div> <!-- End card -->
  </div>
</div> <!-- End row-->
```

7. Update the `styles` property from our component to the following:

```
styles: [`
  img.avatar {
    height: 60px;
    width: 60px;
```

```
    }
    span.date {
      font-size: small;
    }
  `],
```

If we refresh our browser now, this is how our page will look:

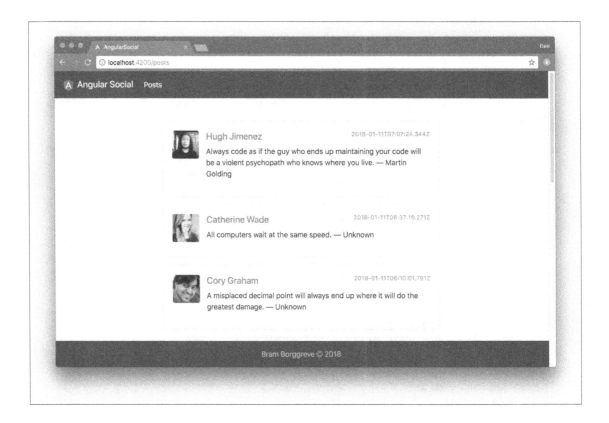

Creating the ProfileItemComponent

We will be using the `ng generate` command to create our `ProfileItemComponent`:

1. Open the `src/app/posts/container/posts/profile.component.ts` file.
2. Update the template to the following:

   ```
   <app-profile-item [profile]="profile"></app-profile-item>
   ```

3. Open your terminal and navigate to the project directory.

4. Run the following command from inside the project directory:

```
ng g c posts/components/profile-item
   create src/app/posts/components/profile-item/profile-item.
component.spec.ts (664 bytes)
   create src/app/posts/components/profile-item/profile-item.component.ts
(273 bytes)
   update src/app/posts/posts.module.ts (846 bytes)
```

5. Open the `src/app/posts/components/profile-item/profile-item.component.ts` file.

6. Import the `Input` from `@angular/core` by adding it to the existing `import` statement.

7. Add the following property in the component class:

```
@Input() profile: any;
```

8. Update the template to the following:

```html
<div class="row">
 <div class="col-md-8 offset-md-2">
   <div class="card mb-3" *ngFor="let post of profile.posts">
     <div class="card-body">
       <div class="media">
         <img class="avatar mr-3 rounded" [attr.src]="profile?.avatar">
         <div class="media-body">
           <h5>
             <a [routerLink]="profile?.id"> {{profile?.fullName}} </a>
             <span class="date float-right text-muted">

             </span>
           </h5>
           <p>{{post?.text}}</p>
         </div>
       </div>
     </div>
   </div>
 </div>
</div>
```

9. Update the `styles` property from our component to the following:

```
styles: [`
  img.avatar {
    height: 60px;
```

```
      width: 60px;
    }
    span.date {
      font-size: small;
    }
  `],
```

When we now refresh the application in our browser, we see that the content is styled and that the navigation still works as expected:

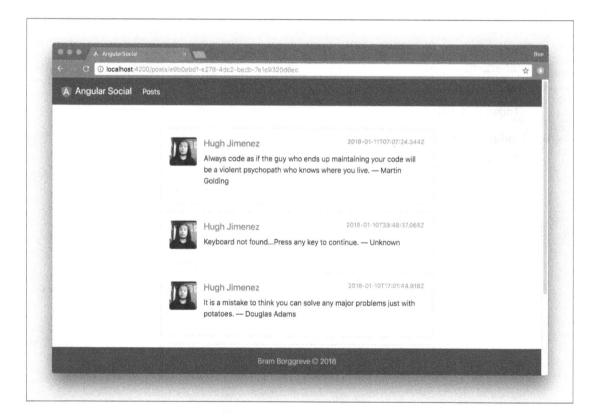

We have successfully separated the concerns of retrieving the data and displaying it.

It's generally a good idea to keep components as small and simple as possible; in particular, our `PostItemComponent` could probably be split up into multiple components.

For our purpose, this works perfectly and we can continue with our last step in this lesson, which is to properly handle retrieving our data using the Angular router.

Creating Resolvers to Retrieve Data Using the Router

In this section, we will manually create two Injectable classes that act as resolvers and then configure our router to use these resolvers. We will then update our container components to use this resolved data.

A resolver is a class that we can use to fetch the data that we use in our component *before* the component is displayed. We call the resolvers in the routes where we need the data. In our implementation, the resolvers retrieve the data from the API and return it so it can be displayed in the components.

> More information about resolvers can be found at:
> `https://angular.io/guide/router#resolve-pre-fetching-component-data`.

Our application is quite neatly structured already, but there is one thing that we can optimize.

In order to see what our problem is, open Chrome Developer Tools and then the **Performance** tab:

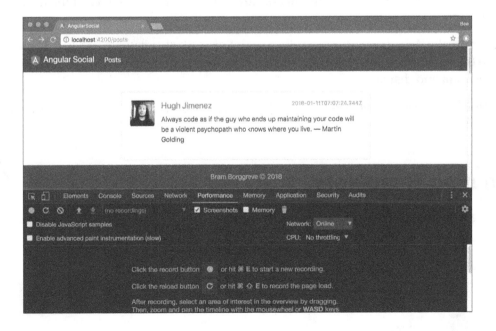

Hit the cog icon and set **Network** to **Slow 3G**:

If we now click around in our application, we will see that that our page navigation still works, but we are presented with empty pages.

The reason for this is that while our components are loaded correctly, they still need to retrieve the data after they are loaded. This is because our components call into the PostsService from our ngOnInit method.

It would be better if our router could make sure that the component has all the needed data loaded before entering the page.

Fortunately, the Angular router provides a way to handle this using resolvers. They will resolve the data before entering the route, and in our component, we can just take this resolved data and display it.

The resolvers that we create need the @Injectable() decorator to make sure they are part of the dependency injection in Angular.

Creating Resolvers

Now we will create a resolver that resolves our post:

1. Open a terminal and run the following command:

   ```
   ng g class posts/resolvers/posts-resolver
   ```

2. Open the `src/app/posts/resolvers/posts-resolver.ts` file.

3. Start the file by defining the needed imports:

```
import { Injectable } from '@angular/core'
import { Resolve } from '@angular/router'
import { PostsService } from '../services/posts.service'
```

4. Decorate the `PostsResolver` class with the `@Injectable` operator:

```
@Injectable()
export class PostsResolver {}
```

5. Make the class implement `Resolve<any>`:

```
@Injectable()
export class PostsResolver implements Resolve<any> {
}
```

6. Inside the class, create a constructor and inject our `PostsService`:

```
constructor(private postsService: PostsService) {}
```

7. Below the constructor, create a class method called `resolve` and make it return the `getPosts()` method from our `PostsService`:

```
resolve() {
```

```
    return this.postsService.getPosts()
}
```

This is the resolver that will be used to retrieve all our posts, just like how we do this currently in our `PostsComponent`.

Now we will create a resolver that resolves our profile:

1. Open a terminal and run the following command:

    ```
    ng g class posts/resolvers/profile-resolver
    ```

2. Open the `src/app/posts/resolvers/profile-resolver.ts` file.
3. Start the file by defining the needed imports:

    ```
    import { Injectable } from '@angular/core'
    import { ActivatedRouteSnapshot, Resolve } from '@angular/router'
    import { PostsService } from '../services/posts.service'
    ```

4. Decorate the `ProfileResolver` class with the `@Injectable` operator:

    ```
    @Injectable()
    export class ProfileResolver {}
    ```

5. Make the class implement `Resolve<any>`:

    ```
    @Injectable()
    export class ProfileResolver implements Resolve<any> {
    }
    ```

6. Inside the class, create a constructor and inject our `PostsService`:

    ```
    constructor(private postsService: PostsService) {}
    ```

7. Below the constructor, create a class method called `resolve`, and pass the `route:
    ActivatedRouteSnapshot` class into it:

    ```
    resolve(route: ActivatedRouteSnapshot) {
    }
    ```

8. Inside the `resolve` method, we return the `getProfile()` method from our
    `PostsService` while getting the `params['profileid']` off our route:

    ```
    resolve(route: ActivatedRouteSnapshot) {
      return this.postsService.getProfile(route.params['profileId'])
    }
    ```

This is the resolver that will be used to retrieve the posts that we have navigated to in our
route.

Importing Our Resolvers

We will add our two new resolvers to the `PostsRoutingModule`. We do this by importing
the resolvers and then adding a `resolve` property to both of our routes. The `resolve`
property takes an object where the key is how the data will be available in the router after it
is resolved, and the value is a reference to the imported resolver:

1. Open the `src/app/posts/posts-routing.module.ts` file.

2. Import our two freshly created resolvers:

    ```
    import { PostsResolver } from './resolvers/posts-resolver'
    import { ProfileResolver } from './resolvers/profile-resolver'
    ```

3. Update both our routes to add a `resolve` property and call to the resolvers:

    ```
    { path: '', component: PostsComponent, resolve: { posts: PostsResolver }
    },
    { path: ':profileId', component: ProfileComponent, resolve: { profile:
    ProfileResolver } },
    ```

When we now refresh our page, we see that we get no output displayed and that we have an error in the browser console:

In order to fix this error, we need to *provide* the resolvers in our module, just like how we do it with other Injectables, such as services:

1. Open the `src/app/posts/posts.module.ts` file.

2. Import the two resolvers:

```
import { PostsResolver } from './resolvers/posts-resolver'
import { ProfileResolver } from './resolvers/profile-resolver'
```

3. Add a reference to both resolvers to the `providers` array:

```
providers: [PostsService, PostsResolver, ProfileResolver]
```

When the application refreshes, we see that the error in the console is gone.

If we check in the **Network** tab in Chrome Developer Tools, we see that we make two requests to the same endpoint. This is because we retrieve the data twice, in our resolver and in our component. Let's update our container components and let them use the data resolved by the router.

Using the Data Resolved by the Router

We will update our `PostsComponent` to read the data that has been resolved by our router. We subscribe to the data of the active route and we map over that data twice. In the first map command, the `posts` value relates to the object key we used in our resolver object for this route:

1. Open the `src/app/posts/container/posts/posts.component.ts` file.

2. Import `ActivatedRoute` from `@angular/router`:

   ```
   import { ActivatedRoute } from '@angular/router'
   ```

3. Remove the `PostsService` import as we are no longer going to use it here.

4. Update the constructor to inject `private route: ActivatedRoute`:

   ```
   constructor(private route: ActivatedRoute) { }
   ```

5. Update the `ngOnInit()` method and replace the content as follows:

   ```
   ngOnInit() {
     this.route.data
       .map(data => data['posts'])
       .map(data => data['items'])
       .subscribe((result: any) => this.posts = result)
   }
   ```

6. Because we will always have data available when arriving on the route, we can remove the assignment from our `posts` property, so it looks like this:

   ```
   public posts: any
   ```

Refresh the page and make sure the data is still loaded.

Now, we will update our `ProfileComponent` to read the data that has been resolved by our router. We subscribe to the data of the active route and we map over that data. In our map command, the value `profile` relates to the object key we used in our resolver object for this route:

1. Open the `src/app/posts/container/profile/profile.component.ts` file.

2. Remove the `PostsService` import as we are no longer going to use it here.

3. Update the constructor to only inject `private route: ActivatedRoute`:

   ```
   constructor(private route: ActivatedRoute) { }
   ```

4. Update the `ngOnInit()` method and replace the content as follows:

```
this.route.data
  .map(data => data['profile'])
  .subscribe((result: any) => this.profile = result)
```

5. Remove the assignment from the `public profile` property so it looks like this:

```
public profile: any;
```

And we are done! Our basic application is built and even though there are enough things to add and optimize, it's well-structured and works using Angular's best practices.

In this section, we created our container components and added dummy data. We also created presentational components and implemented resolvers for our app. In the next lesson, we will add support for server-side rendering by adding Angular Universal.

Summary

In this lesson, we learned the different types of components and how to create them. We then learned how to create resolvers to retrieve data using the router.

In the next lesson, we will look at implementing server-side rendering in our app.

3

Server-Side Rendering

How does a normal app render?

Let's first take a look at how a normal Angular application without server-side rendering behaves.

When we start our server in development mode, using `ng serve`, and we use the **View Source** option in our browser to check the source, we see that the only thing that gets rendered is the output from our `src/index.html` file, with a few scripts appended at the bottom.

These scripts will be downloaded by the browser and after they have been downloaded and executed, the application will display:

While this works in some situations, in others this can become problematic. If the user of your app is on a slow connection or slow device, it will take time to load and parse the scripts, and during that waiting time, the user sees a blank page.

Another issue is that most search engines and social media sites will only read the initial *payload* of our website and will not download and execute our client-side JavaScript files.

These are the things that will be fixed in this lesson. After we have added server-side rendering, we will add support for dynamic metadata and page titles. This makes sure that any server-side rendered page has proper metadata, which will make these social pages rich in content and will make sure that search engines can index the pages properly.

To get the actual loading times, use the status bar of the **Network** tab in Chrome Developer Tools.

One way to experience a slow connection on a normal Chrome browser is to open Chrome Developer Tools, go to the **Network** tab, and change the network speed from **Online** to **Slow 3G**. When you load the page served by the server, you will get an idea of how long it takes for a slow connection to load the application:

Lesson Objectives

In this lesson, you will:

- Add server-side rendering to the application that we built in the previous lesson
- Add Angular Universal to our application and configure a second app in our Angular CLI config
- Implement a web server to host our app
- Add dynamic metadata to our application

Generating the Server App

Since Angular CLI version 1.6, there has been a generator for adding support for Angular Universal. It does this by adding a second app to the Angular CLI config, `.angular-cli.json`.

We will refer to this new app as our *server app*, and the one we worked with in the previous lesson will be called our *browser app*.

So, what are the differences between the browser and server apps?

- Both load another platform which behaves differently.
- The browser app uses code splitting, which builds the app in various smaller files. This improves load times in the browser. The server builds the app without code splitting as there are no benefits to do this on the server.
- The browser app loads a greater number of polyfills. These are small JavaScript libraries that add functionality to the browser, if the browser does not support them yet. This is not needed for the server.

Let's explore in some more detail what happens when we run the generator:

```
~/dev/angular-social master 5m 30s
> ng generate universal server
  create src/app/app.server.module.ts (318 bytes)
  create src/main.server.ts (59 bytes)
  create src/tsconfig.server.json (308 bytes)
  update package.json (1367 bytes)
  update .angular-cli.json (1980 bytes)
  update src/main.ts (430 bytes)
  update src/app/app.module.ts (608 bytes)

~/dev/angular-social master*
> npm install
added 3 packages in 7.796s

~/dev/angular-social master* 8s
>
```

Running this generator will change a few things in the current app:

- It will add a second app to the `apps` array in `.angular-cli.json`.
- It will add a dependency for the `@angular/platform-server` package.
- It will update `AppModule` and change the `BrowserModule` import.
- It will change the way the browser app gets bootstrapped in `src/main.ts`.

Additionally, it creates some new files:

- It generates a new file `src/app/app.server.module.ts` with the `AppServerModule`
- The `src/main.server.ts` file is created, which exports the `AppServerModule`
- A TypeScript config file for the server app is generated in `src/tsconfig.server.json`

As stated above, we have new dependencies in `package.json`. This means we need to run `npm install` to make sure the dependencies get installed.

Generating the Angular Universal Application

We will create the server app and install the missing dependencies:

1. Open the terminal in the project directory.
2. Run the generator to add the Universal app. The command is as follows:

   `ng generate universal server`

3. Install the dependencies that were added to `package.json`:

   `npm install`

Making Our Apps Consistent

We will make some small changes to both the browser app and the server app so that they are more consistent:

1. Open the terminal in the project directory.
2. Run the following command to update the `outDir` of the server app:

   `ng set apps.1.outDir=dist/server`

3. Run the following command to update the `outDir` of the browser app:

```
ng set apps.0.outDir=dist/browser
```

4. Run the following command to update the `name` of the browser app:

```
ng set apps.0.name=browser
```

5. Run the following command to update the `platform` of the browser app:

```
ng set apps.0.platform=browser
```

```
~/dev/angular-social master*
) ng set apps.1.outDir=dist/server

~/dev/angular-social master*
) ng set apps.0.outDir=dist/browser

~/dev/angular-social master*
) ng set apps.0.name=browser

~/dev/angular-social master*
) ng set apps.0.platform=browser

~/dev/angular-social master*
)
```

The changes will be reflected in `.angular-cli.json`:

```
  "apps": [
    {
+     "name": "browser",
      "root": "src",
-     "outDir": "dist",
+     "outDir": "dist/browser",
      "assets": [
        "assets",
        "favicon.ico"
      ],
+     "platform": "browser",
      "index": "index.html",
      "main": "main.ts",
      "polyfills": "polyfills.ts",
@@ -29,12 +31,14 @@
    }
    },
    {
+     "name": "server",
      "root": "src",
-     "outDir": "dist-server/",
+     "outDir": "dist/server",
      "assets": [
        "assets",
```

We've now installed the required dependencies.

In this section, we have created a new server app in addition to the browser app we already had. Let's move on to adding support for Angular Universal in our application.

Adding Dependencies for the Server App

In order to get our server app working correctly, we need to make sure we load two of Angular's dependencies: `zone.js` and `reflect-metadata`.

Our browser app loads these dependencies using `polyfills.ts`, and for the server app, we will add them to `src/main.server.ts`.

Another dependency that we need to add is the `ModuleMapLoaderModule`. This is a third-party module that is needed to make Angular Universal apps work with lazy loading.

We will import two dependencies in `src/main.server.ts` so that they are imported when the `AppServerModule` is loaded.

Additionally, we will enable production mode, just like it's done for the browser app in `src/main.ts`:

1. Open the newly created file `src/main.server.ts`.

2. Add the imports at the top of the file:

```
import 'zone.js/dist/zone-node';
import 'reflect-metadata';

import { enableProdMode } from '@angular/core';
import { environment } from './environments/environment';
```

3. Conditionally enable production mode, depending on the environment:

```
if (environment.production) {
  enableProdMode();
}
```

Let's move on to adding this new application to our Angular CLI configuration!

Adding the Server App to Our Angular CLI Configuration

1. Open a terminal inside the project directory.

2. Run the following command to install the dependency:

   ```
   npm install --save @nguniversal/module-map-ngfactory-loader
   ```

3. Open the `src/app/app.server.module.ts` file in your editor.

4. Add the following `import` at the top of the file:

   ```
   import { ModuleMapLoaderModule } from '@nguniversal/module-map-
   ngfactory-loader';
   ```

5. Add a reference to the imported module to the `imports` array:

   ```
   imports: [
     ...
     ModuleMapLoaderModule,
   ],
   ```

In this section, we added the required dependencies and added the server app to our configuration. In the next section, let's explore run scripts and add them to our application.

Adding Run Scripts to package.json

Now that we have added a second application to our Angular CLI config, we need to make sure we can easily build both applications without having to memorize the exact commands.

In order to do so, we will leverage the so-called npm scripts. These scripts are used to define operations that can be performed on our application. Examples of these operations are building the application, running tests, and deploying the application to a staging or production environment.

We can define our npm scripts in the `scripts` section of the `package.json` file in the root of our project.

Here, we will add three scripts called `build`, `build:browser`, and `build:server`, where the first script will invoke the other two.

This gives us the flexibility to run the two commands at once, or run them independently if we like.

To get an idea of how these scripts work, consider the following flow:

1. The `npm run build` command will first run `npm run build:browser`.
2. When that command is finished, it will run `npm run build:server`.

The order in which we run the `build:browser` and `build:server` scripts is irrelevant; the scripts are fully independent.

Adding npm Scripts

We will add some npm scripts to our `package.json` so we can easily create builds for our application:

1. Open the `package.json` file from the root of our project in the editor.
2. Locate the `scripts` object and remove the existing `build` property.
3. Add the following keys to the `scripts` object:

```
"build": "npm run build:browser && npm run build:server",
"build:browser": "ng build --prod --app browser",
"build:server": "ng build --prod --app server --output-hashing=false",
```

Testing the Builds of Both Apps

We will test the builds of both the browser and server applications:

1. Open a terminal inside the project directory.
2. Run the following command to build the browser application:

```
$ npm run build:browser
```

```
●  ●  ●                          ~/dev/angular-social

~/dev/angular-social master* ↑
⟩ npm run build:browser

> angular-social@0.0.0 build:browser /Users/beeman/dev/angular-social
> ng build --prod --app browser

Date: 2018-01-11T22:02:52.879Z
Hash: 863c83d53c3dc76ba908
Time: 18356ms
chunk {0} 0.170fabbe8d614e24943a.chunk.js () 9.06 kB  [rendered]
chunk {1} polyfills.abdf53ca655716e505e0.bundle.js (polyfills) 59.2 kB [initial] [rendered]
chunk {2} main.5c910bbfcc9a982516f0.bundle.js (main) 265 kB [initial] [rendered]
chunk {3} styles.6059536c9ecc1eb1f4ba.bundle.css (styles) 258 bytes [initial] [rendered]
chunk {4} inline.64e1b3cb7b22d4c98b6e.bundle.js (inline) 1.47 kB [entry] [rendered]

~/dev/angular-social master* ↑ 21s
⟩ ▊
```

3. Run the following command to build the server application:

```
$ npm run build:server
```

```
●  ●  ●                          ~/dev/angular-social

~/dev/angular-social master* ↑
⟩ npm run build:server

> angular-social@0.0.0 build:server /Users/beeman/dev/angular-social
> ng build --prod --app server --output-hashing=false

Date: 2018-01-11T22:04:43.758Z
Hash: f23a4cf8f5a90f574bfe
Time: 4912ms
chunk {0} main.bundle.js (main) 30.7 kB [entry] [rendered]
chunk {1} polyfills.bundle.js (polyfills) 788 bytes [entry] [rendered]
chunk {2} styles.bundle.css (styles) 258 bytes [entry] [rendered]

~/dev/angular-social master* ↑ 7s
⟩ ▊
```

If both commands execute without any error messages, we can continue with our next step, which is implementing a small web server to host our application.

Implementing a Web Server

Now that both our applications can be built, we can move on to creating a simple server to host our applications.

In order to do this, we will create a simple Node.js server based on Express.js.

We will define our server in a TypeScript file called `server.ts` and run this file using the `ts-node` binary that we will install.

The current implementation of Angular Universal depends on Node.js as it is implemented in JavaScript.

It is possible to run Angular Universal apps using other servers, such as ASP.NET, although under the hood the ASP.NET server will invoke a Node.js process to handle the Angular Universal part.

An example repository of how to run Angular Universal can be found here: `https://github.com/MarkPieszak/aspnetcore-angular2-universal`.

Installing Server Dependencies

We will install the `ts-node` binary that we will use to execute our server file. Additionally, we will install the rendering engine that will be used by Express.js to load our Angular Universal app:

1. Open a terminal inside the project directory.
2. Run the following command to install `ts-node`:

   ```
   npm install --save ts-node @nguniversal/express-engine
   ```

```
~/dev/angular-social master* ↑ 42s
> npm install --save ts-node @nguniversal/express-engine
+ ts-node@3.2.2
+ @nguniversal/express-engine@5.0.0-beta.5
added 1 package and updated 1 package in 6.744s

~/dev/angular-social master* ↑ 7s
>
```

Creating the server.ts File

We will implement our `server.ts` file.

In this file, we will define our Express.js server and configure it so it can render and serve our server app:

1. In your editor, create a new file called `server.ts` in the project root.

2. Add the following `import` statements at the top of the file:
   ```
   import * as express from 'express';
   import { join } from 'path';
   import { ngExpressEngine } from '@nguniversal/express-engine';
   import { provideModuleMap } from '@nguniversal/module-map-ngfactory-
   loader';
   ```

3. Define the constants that we will use in the server:
   ```
   const PORT = process.env.PORT || 8080;
   const staticRoot = join(process.cwd(), 'dist', 'browser');
   const { AppServerModuleNgFactory, LAZY_MODULE_MAP } = require('./dist/
   server/main.bundle');
   const app = express();
   ```

4. Define the `html` view engine. This will let Express.js know which function it uses to render HTML files:
   ```
   app.engine('html', ngExpressEngine({
     bootstrap: AppServerModuleNgFactory,
     providers: [
       provideModuleMap(LAZY_MODULE_MAP)
     ]
   ```

```
}));
```

5. Define the rest of the Express.js defaults. We set our default view engine to `html`, the engine we defined in the previous step. Next, we set the root directory for our views to reference our `staticRoot`:

```
app.set('view engine', 'html');
app.set('views', staticRoot);
```

6. With the following Express.js defaults, we define that we want to statically serve all other files than of type `html`, and that the default route (*) is to render the `index.html` file:

```
app.get('*.*', express.static(staticRoot));
app.get('*', (req, res) => res.render('index', { req }));
```

7. Start the server and log a message with the host and port:

```
app.listen(PORT, () => console.log(`Server listening on http://
localhost:${PORT}`));
```

Adding the npm Script to package.json

We will update `package.json` and add a script to start our server:

1. Open the `package.json` file in the root of our project in the editor.
2. Locate the `scripts` object and remove the existing `start` property.
3. Add the following key to the `scripts` object:

```
"start": "ts-node ./server",
```

Starting the Server

We will build and start our app, and test whether it works!

1. Run the complete build using the following command:

```
$ npm run build
```

2. Start the Node.js server using the following command:

```
$ npm start
```

```
● ● ●                                    angular-social: npm start

~/dev/angular-social master* ↑ 29s
) npm start

> angular-social@0.0.0 start /Users/beeman/dev/angular-social
> ts-node ./server

Server listening on http://localhost:8080
```

3. Navigate to the server-side rendered build at: `http://localhost:8080`.

4. Verify that the application works.

5. From the Chrome menu, go to **View** | **Developer Tools** | **View Source** and verify that the application output gets rendered.

In this section, we ran our app on a server built using Express.js. The next step is to add dynamic metadata, which will help our app become more SEO-friendly.

Adding Dynamic Metadata

Now that our pages can be rendered using server-side rendering, we can introduce new functionality to enhance the appearance of our app.

At the moment, our app will still only display the default title set in `src/index.html` and we won't have any other HTML meta tags added.

To enhance the SEO friendliness of our page, and to make sure there is valuable information in our social preview, we want to address this.

Luckily, Angular comes with the `Meta` and `Title` classes, which allow us to add dynamic titles and metadata to our pages.

When combined with server-side rendering, the metadata and page title will make sure that the pages that are indexed by the search engine have the proper meta tags set in the document header, and thus increase findability.

In this section, we will add a service that allows us to define this data, and we will update our container components to call in that service after the data is loaded from our resolvers.

Creating the UiService

1. Open a terminal inside the project directory.

2. Run the following command to generate the `UiService` and register it in the `UiModule`:

    ```
    ng g s ui/services/ui --module ui/ui
    ```

    ```
    ● ● ●                                    ~/dev/angular-social
    ~/dev/angular-social master*
    ) ng g s ui/services/ui --module ui/ui
      create src/app/ui/services/ui.service.spec.ts (350 bytes)
      create src/app/ui/services/ui.service.ts (108 bytes)
      update src/app/ui/ui.module.ts (596 bytes)

    ~/dev/angular-social master*
    )
    ```

3. Open the `src/app/ui/services/ui.service.ts` file in your editor.

4. Add the following lines to the class definition:

    ```
    private appColor = '#C3002F';
    private appImage = '/assets/logo.svg';
    private appTitle = 'Angular Social';
    private appDescription = 'Angular Social is a Social Networking App
    built in Angular';
    ```

5. Import `Title` and `Meta` from `@angular/platform-browser`:

    ```
    import { Meta, Title } from '@angular/platform-browser';
    ```

6. Inject `private title: Title` and `private meta: Meta` in the constructor:

    ```
    constructor(private titleService: Title, private metaService: Meta) {}
    ```

7. Add a class method called `setMetaData` that takes in a property `config`:

    ```
    public setMetaData(config) {}
    ```

8. Add the following code to the body of the `setMetaData` property:

    ```
    // Get the description of the config, or use the default App Description
    const description = config.description || this.appDescription
    // Get the title of the config and append the App Title, or just use the
    App Title
    ```

```
const title = config.title ? `${config.title} - ${this.appTitle}` :
this.appTitle;

// Set the Application Title
this.titleService.setTitle(title);

// Add the Application Meta tags
this.metaService.addTags([
    { name: 'description', content: description },
    { name: 'theme-color', content: this.appColor },
    { name: 'twitter:card', content: 'summary' },
    { name: 'twitter:image', content: this.appImage },
    { name: 'twitter:title', content: title },
    { name: 'twitter:description', content: description },
    { name: 'apple-mobile-web-app-capable', content: 'yes' },
    { name: 'apple-mobile-web-app-status-bar-style', content: 'black-
translucent' },
    { name: 'apple-mobile-web-app-title', content: title },
    { name: 'apple-touch-startup-image', content: this.appImage },
    { property: 'og:title', content: title },
    { property: 'og:description', content: description },
    { property: 'og:image', content: this.appImage },
]);
```

Our `UiService` is now ready to be used. We will start by adding it to the components in our next section.

Adding Metadata to PostsComponent and ProfileComponent

We will add the metadata to the `PostsComponent`:

1. Open the `src/app/posts/container/posts/posts.component.ts` file in your editor.

2. Import the `UiService` and the `map` operator from `rxjs`:

    ```
    import { UiService } from '../../../ui/services/ui.service';
    ```

3. Inside the constructor, inject `private uiService: UiService`:

    ```
    constructor(private route: ActivatedRoute, private uiService: UiService)
    { }
    ```

4. Add a class method called `setMetadata()` that accepts a `posts` property:

```
setMetaData(posts) {}
```

5. Add the following to the `setMetaData` method. In this method, we will construct the dynamic metadata that we will pass to our `setMetaData` method in the `UiService`:

```
const { itemsPerPage, itemsTotal } = posts['counters']
const description = `Showing ${itemsPerPage} from ${itemsTotal} posts`
const title = 'Posts List'

this.uiService.setMetaData({ description, title })
return posts;
```

6. Update the first `map` statement in the `ngOnInit` method to the following code. This will pass the data we get from the API through the method we defined above:

```
.map(data => this.setMetaData(data['posts']))
```

Now we will add the metadata to the `ProfileComponent`:

1. Open the `src/app/posts/container/profile/profile.component.ts` file in your editor.

2. Import the `UiService` and the `map` operator from `rxjs`:

```
import { UiService } from '../../../ui/services/ui.service';
```

3. Inside the constructor, inject `private uiService: UiService`:

```
constructor(private route: ActivatedRoute, private uiService: UiService)
{ }
```

4. Add a class method called `setMetadata()` that accepts a property `profile`:

```
setMetaData(profile) {}
```

5. Add the following to the `setMetaData` method. In this method, we will construct the dynamic metadata that we will pass to our `setMetaData` method in the `UiService`:

```
const { fullName, posts } = profile;
const description = `${fullName} posted ${posts.length} posts.`;
const title = `Posts by ${fullName}`;
this.uiService.setMetaData({ description, title });
return profile;
```

6. Update the `ngOnInit` method to the following code. This will pass the data we get from the API through the method we defined above:

```
this.route.data
    .map(data => this.setMetaData(data['profile']))
    .subscribe((result: any) => this.profile = result)
```

When you now browse through the application, you should see the title of the page update, depending on the page you are visiting.

You can use the **Element Inspector** in Chrome Developer Tools to verify that the metadata is being added to the rendered components:

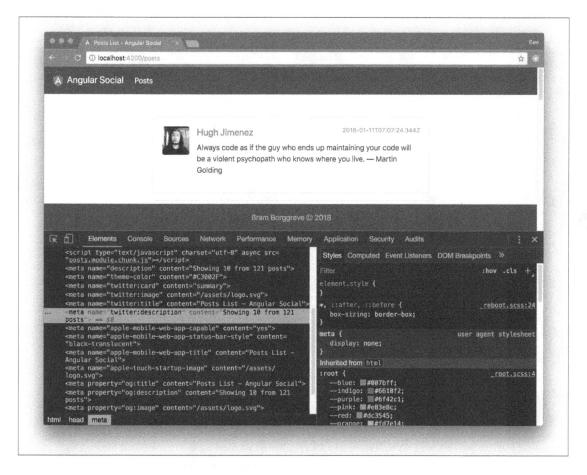

In this section, we have added metadata to our `PostsComponent` and `ProfileComponent`. We also created a UiService that allows us to define this data.

Summary

In this lesson, we have added server-side rendering to our application. We started by generating the server app and adding its dependencies. We then added scripts to our `package.json` file, before implementing a web server in Express.js. Lastly, we saw how to add dynamic metadata to our pages.

In the next lesson, we'll configure service workers for our application.

4

Service Workers

In the previous lesson, we learned how to add server-side rendering to our application. In the next lesson, we'll configure service workers for our application.

Lesson Objectives

In this lesson, you will:

- Explore service workers and PWAs
- Add a service worker to the application that we built in the previous lessons
- Configure the service worker to convert the app to a progressive web app
- Explore how to debug a service worker

Let's first understand what a service worker and a progressive web app is.

What Is a Service Worker?

A service worker is a script that the browser runs in the background which acts as a network proxy to manage network requests programmatically. It sits between the network and the device and caches content, enabling an offline experience for the user.

In addition to caching data, it can also synchronize API data in the background and add things like push notifications.

What Is a Progressive Web App?

Progressive Web App (PWA) is a term that is used for web applications that behave in a way similar to native mobile applications.

Like native apps, they allow an application to be started when the user is offline, caching the UI elements and API calls to display an initial page. That way, a user can interact with the application on a basic level until the connection gets established.

Once the connection is established, the PWA will retrieve the updated data from the server and refresh the application, so the user can work with the latest data.

 The official Angular documentation has a great section on service workers: `https://angular.io/guide/service-worker-intro`

Installing Dependencies

Angular comes with support for service workers. In order to use it, we first need to install the dependencies.

1. Open the terminal in the project directory.

2. Install the dependencies needed using the `npm` command:

   `npm install @angular/service-worker`

3. When the installation is successful, we should see the new package added to the `dependencies` object in our project's `package.json` file:

```
~/dev/angular-social master
> npm install @angular/service-worker
npm WARN @schematics/angular@0.1.12 requires a peer of @angular-devkit/schematics@0.0.43 but none is
  installed. You must install peer dependencies yourself.

+ @angular/service-worker@5.2.0
added 1 package in 7.678s

~/dev/angular-social master* 8s
>
```

In this section, we have installed the dependencies for our service worker, which is the first step in implementing service workers in our app. Let's move on to the next section, where we will enable the service worker in our application.

Enabling the Service Worker

Now that the dependency is installed, it's time to enable the service worker.

This involves three steps:

1. Enabling the service worker in our browser app in `.angular-cli.json`.
2. Importing and registering the `ServiceWorkerModule` in our `AppModule`.
3. Creating the service worker configuration file `src/ngsw-config.json`.

We will use the `ng set` command to enable support for the service worker in our browser app in `.angular-cli.json`:

1. Open the terminal in the project directory.
2. Run the following command to adjust `.angular-cli.json`:

   ```
   ng set apps.0.serviceWorker=true
   ```

3. Confirm that the property `serviceWorker` is set to `true` in the first app in the `apps` array in `.angular-cli.json`:

Importing the ServiceWorkerModule

We will import the `ServiceWorkerModule` in our `AppModule` and register it.

We will invoke the `register` method on the `ServiceWorkerModule`. This method takes two parameters. The first parameter defines what the location of the Angular service worker is. The value `'/ngsw-worker.js'` is what should be used in our case.

The second parameter is an object named `environment`, and with this object, we can control if we want to enable the service worker. We use the `environment` object to determine if the service worker should be enabled, as we only want to enable it on production builds:

1. Open the `src/app/app.module.ts` file in your editor.
2. Add the following `import` statements at the top of the file:

```
import { ServiceWorkerModule } from '@angular/service-worker'
import { environment } from '../environments/environment'
```

Add the `ServiceWorkerModule` to the `imports` array and invoke the `register` method with these parameters:

```
ServiceWorkerModule.register('/ngsw-worker.js', {enabled: environment.
production}),
```

Creating the Service Worker Configuration

1. Create the `src/ngsw-config.json` file and open it in your editor.
2. Add the following content to the file:

```
{
  "index": "/index.html",
  "assetGroups": [
    {
      "name": "app",
      "installMode": "prefetch",
      "resources": {
        "files": [
          "/favicon.ico",
          "/index.html"
        ],
        "versionedFiles": [
          "/*.bundle.css",
```

```
        "/*.bundle.js",
        "/*.chunk.js"
      ]
    }
  },
  {
    "name": "assets",
    "installMode": "lazy",
    "updateMode": "prefetch",
    "resources": {
      "files": [
        "/assets/**"
      ]
    }
  }
  ]
}
```

Here, we add the initial default content to the `ngsw-config.json` file. This is the default configuration provided by the Angular team, and can be found here: `https://angular.io/guide/service-worker-getting-started#step-4-create-the-configuration-file-ngsw-configjson`

1. Open the Terminal in the project directory.

2. Run `npm run build:browser` to create a production build.

3. Verify that the build ran successfully and that the files `ngsw-worker.js` and `ngsw.json` got generated in the `dist/browser` directory.

In this section, we enabled the service worker in our application and used the default configuration. We have verified that a production build generates the service worker configuration.

Let's add some custom configuration options next.

Configuring the Service Worker

In the previous section, we added the service worker configuration file `src/ngsw-config.json` to our project, but we have not configured anything yet.

In this section, we will add two types of configurations: asset groups and data groups.

Asset and Data Groups

In the asset groups configuration, we specify how we want our service worker to handle the assets of our application. When we talk about assets, we should think of style sheets, images, external JS files, and so on.

Asset groups are defined using the following TypeScript interface:

```
interface AssetGroup {
  name: string;
  installMode?: 'prefetch' | 'lazy';
```

```
  updateMode?: 'prefetch' | 'lazy';
  resources: {
    files?: string[];
    versionedFiles?: string[];
    urls?: string[];
  };
}
```

Here's what the parameters mean:

- `name` uniquely identifies the group of assets
- `installMode` defines how new resources are initially cached
- `updateMode` defines the caching behavior of existing resources
- The `resources` object describes the actual resource to cache

A complete reference for this can be found at:
`https://angular.io/guide/service-worker-config#assetgroups`.

In the data groups configuration, we specify how we want our service worker to cache the data of the APIs we are requesting the data from.

Data groups are defined using the following TypeScript interface:

```
export interface DataGroup {
  name: string;
  urls: string[];
  version?: number;
  cacheConfig: {
    maxSize: number;
    maxAge: string;
    timeout?: string;
    strategy?: 'freshness' | 'performance';
  };
};
```

Here's what the parameters mean:

- `name` uniquely identifies the group
- `urls` is an array of URL patterns
- `version` provides a mechanism to force reloading of cached items
- `cacheConfig` defines the policy that is used to cache this group

A complete reference for this can be found at:
`https://angular.io/guide/service-worker-config#datagroups`.

Configuring the Asset and Data Groups

We will append two items to the asset groups configuration.

The first asset group caches the data that comes from the domains that we use to fetch our CSS and the fonts included in that CSS.

The second asset group caches the static data from the API we work with; in this case, the user avatars:

1. Open the `src/ngsw-config.json` file in your editor.
2. Locate the `assetGroups` array.
3. Add the following two objects to this array:

```json
{
    "name": "externals",
    "installMode": "prefetch",
    "updateMode": "prefetch",
    "resources": {
      "urls": [
        "https://ajax.googleapis.com/**",
        "https://fonts.googleapis.com/**",
        "https://fonts.gstatic.com/**",
        "https://maxcdn.bootstrapcdn.com/**"
      ]
    }
  },
  {
    "name": "avatars",
    "installMode": "prefetch",
    "updateMode": "prefetch",
    "resources": {
      "urls": [
        "http://localhost:3000/avatars/**",
        "https://packt-angular-social.now.sh/avatars/**"
      ]
    }
  }
```

Make sure to correctly format the JSON; use `https://jsonlint.com/` to be sure.

We will create the data groups configuration. We will define one data group that caches the requests from our API:

1. Open the `src/ngsw-config.json` file in your editor.

2. Create a top-level array with the key `dataGroups`.

3. Add the following object to this array:

```json
{
    "name": "rest-api",
    "urls": [
      "http://localhost:3000/api/**",
      "https://packt-angular-social.now.sh/api/**"
    ],
    "cacheConfig": {
      "strategy": "freshness",
      "maxSize": 100,
      "maxAge": "1h",
      "timeout": "5s"
    }
}
```

In this section, we configured the asset groups and data groups of our application in our service worker.

With this configuration and our service worker running, we should be able to retrieve a fully styled application that displays the latest API data.

Testing the Service Worker

In order to test if our service worker works, we will have to load our application, and then disconnect our browser from the internet.

Checking Where the Data Comes from

Using Chrome Developer Tools, it's easy to see where a particular resource is being retrieved from.

Using the **Network** tab in Chrome Developer Tools, you can see what files are being retrieved, where the data comes from, and how long it took the browser to fetch those resources.

The following screenshot shows a normal page request, where each file is downloaded from the web server:

Name	Status	Type	Initiator	Size	Time	Waterfall	5.00 s ▲
localhost	200	document	Other	(from disk cache)	3 ms		
styles.561c1341f19c45b8a584.bundle.css	200	stylesheet	(index)	512 B	22 ms		
inline.7caeb1bdb7de22ae0f8a.bundle.js	200	script	(index)	1.7 KB	23 ms		
polyfills.a5a4fd3436618a8a5a2f.bundle.js	200	script	(index)	59.8 KB	23 ms		
main.c5d62395fd3b2eb4355d.bundle.js	200	script	(index)	288 KB	23 ms		
bootstrap.min.css	200	stylesheet	(index)	22.1 KB	225 ms		
font-awesome.min.css	200	stylesheet	(index)	7.9 KB	434 ms		
0.e66131e720c6a3a756c6.chunk.js	200	script	inline.7cae...	7.1 KB	16 ms		
timeline?filter[where][type]=text	200	xhr	polyfills.a5a...	2.5 KB	286 ms		
e9b0ebd1-e278-4dc2-bedb-7e1e9320d6...	200	jpeg	main.c5d62...	4.6 KB	453 ms		
c83b1e6e-e67d-4f6b-a120-f7faf7ae6371...	200	jpeg	main.c5d62...	5.7 KB	264 ms		
38bbb7ac-d244-43e4-9bb4-78579591e1...	200	jpeg	main.c5d62...	4.0 KB	488 ms		
13c7c2f3-41bb-404a-b1c6-69394af5d62...	200	jpeg	main.c5d62...	9.4 KB	710 ms		
4e2a177a-d197-4148-8c1e-dde93231fa2...	200	jpeg	main.c5d62...	6.8 KB	931 ms		
8f4f6d4d-9c7f-401b-a6fa-f5347134c265.jpg	200	jpeg	main.c5d62...	4.7 KB	711 ms		
10dd19f7-53ef-4fb7-a531-02f1496ab69f.j...	200	jpeg	main.c5d62...	3.2 KB	488 ms		
c5312ed4-8de0-404c-8686-cba6f22946a...	200	jpeg	main.c5d62...	5.0 KB	487 ms		
996b03b4-2fd1-4b15-bd0f-7f260a70bcd...	200	jpeg	main.c5d62...	3.7 KB	708 ms		
fontawesome-webfont.woff2?v=4.7.0	200	font	Other	75.8 KB	881 ms		
ngsw-worker.js	200	javascript	:8080/ngsw...	0 B	19 ms		
ngsw.json?ngsw-cache-bust=0.72685...	200	fetch	ngsw-work...	2.5 KB	4 ms		

In the following screenshot, in the **Size** column, you can see that the data is being retrieved from the service worker. This means it did not make a request to the network to fetch those items; rather, it got them from the browser cache:

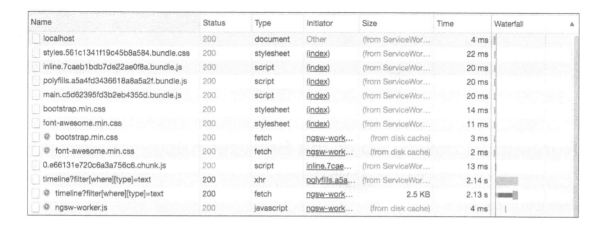

Name	Status	Type	Initiator	Size	Time	Waterfall ▲
localhost	200	document	Other	(from ServiceWor...	4 ms	
styles.561c1341f19c45b8a584.bundle.css	200	stylesheet	(index)	(from ServiceWor...	22 ms	
inline.7caeb1bdb7de22ae0f8a.bundle.js	200	script	(index)	(from ServiceWor...	20 ms	
polyfills.a5a4fd3436618a8a5a2f.bundle.js	200	script	(index)	(from ServiceWor...	20 ms	
main.c5d62395fd3b2eb4355d.bundle.js	200	script	(index)	(from ServiceWor...	20 ms	
bootstrap.min.css	200	stylesheet	(index)	(from ServiceWor...	14 ms	
font-awesome.min.css	200	stylesheet	(index)	(from ServiceWor...	11 ms	
⚙ bootstrap.min.css	200	fetch	ngsw-work...	(from disk cache)	3 ms	
⚙ font-awesome.min.css	200	fetch	ngsw-work...	(from disk cache)	2 ms	
0.e66131e720c6a3a756c6.chunk.js	200	script	inline.7cae...	(from ServiceWor...	13 ms	
timeline?filter[where][type]=text	200	xhr	polyfills.a5a...	(from ServiceWor...	2.14 s	
⚙ timeline?filter[where][type]=text	200	fetch	ngsw-work...	2.5 KB	2.13 s	
⚙ ngsw-worker.js	200	javascript	ngsw-work...	(from disk cache)	4 ms	

Enabling Offline Mode

It's the nature of a web browser to be online, but in reality, we've all found ourselves in situations where our device is offline due to a lack of network connectivity.

In order to develop apps that can handle these situations, Chrome offers a so-called **Offline mode**. It will stop the browser from connecting to the network. That way, we can make sure our applications behave as expected.

In the **Network** tab in Chrome Developer Tools, you can find a checkbox named **Offline**, which triggers this behavior:

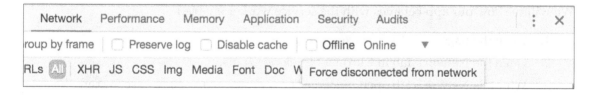

After checking this box, you will see a yellow indicator next to the tab name, which indicates that there is something unusual going on with the **Network** tab:

Running a Local Build of the Browser App

We will build a production version of our app that enables the service worker. Once the build is made, we will host the build using a simple web server called `http-server` and open it in our browser:

1. Build the browser app using the following command:

    ```
    npm run build:browser
    ```

2. Serve the app using the following command:

    ```
    npx http-server ./dist/browser
    ```

    The application will now be served on: `http://localhost:8080`

3. Open the page in the browser. You should see the list of posts.

4. Open the **Console** tab in Chrome Developer Tools and verify that there are no errors.

Inspecting the Behavior

We will see how our app behaves with the service worker enabled:

1. Open the page from the last exercise in the browser.
2. Open the **Network** tab in Chrome Developer Tools.
3. With this **Network** tab open, reload `http://localhost:8080` to see where the data comes from.

You should see that the data gets loaded from the service worker.

Setting Our Application to Offline Mode

We will set our application to **Offline** mode and verify that the service worker displays a complete and cached version of our app:

1. Open the page from the last exercise in the browser.
2. Open the **Network** tab in Chrome Developer Tools.
3. Enable the **Offline** mode by enabling the checkbox.
4. While in **Offline** mode, navigate to: `http://localhost:8080`.

You should see that our application still gets loaded and displays the cached data.

In this section, we ran a local build of our app and then tested its behavior in offline mode. Our app runs well even in offline mode. We can now explore how to debug our service workers.

Debugging the Service Worker

There is a famous saying in computer science:

> *"There are 2 hard problems in computer science: cache invalidation, naming things."*

> *-Phil Karlton*

The first one applies to debugging service workers.

As discussed earlier, a service worker adds a caching layer between the network and the device. This inherently makes it hard to debug, because when you update your service worker definition or the configuration of your website, your changes might very well be cached, and thus not visible.

It is a quite well-known challenge while developing applications with service worker support, so it's good to understand how to debug the service worker.

Chrome Developer Tools to the Rescue

Chrome Developer Tools is an advanced tool for inspecting and debugging the technology behind websites, and luckily, it has great support for service workers.

In the **Application** tab, we can see which service workers are installed, what their status is, and unregister them to make sure we download the latest version.

Locating the Running Service Worker

We will locate where we can find the running service worker:

1. Open the page from the last exercise in the browser.
2. Open the **Application** tab in Chrome Developer Tools.
3. In the sidebar of the **Application** tab, click on the **Service Workers** link.
4. Verify that there is an entry in the list of service workers.

Unregistering the Registered Service Worker

We will unregister our service worker:

1. Open the page from the last exercise in the browser.
2. Open the **Application** tab in Chrome Developer Tools and click on the **Service Workers** link in the sidebar.
3. Locate the entry of the service worker that has the **Status** set to **activated**.
4. Click on the **Unregister** link next to the **Update** link.
5. When you now refresh the page, a new service worker should be loaded.

[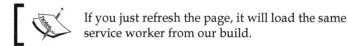 If you just refresh the page, it will load the same service worker from our build.]

The development cycle for building a service worker looks something like this:

1. Make a change in the Angular application.
2. Create a production build using the `npm run build:browser` command.
3. Serve the new build using the `npx http-server ./dist/browser` command.
4. Unregister the currently active service worker.
5. Browse to the new version and verify the changes you made are applied.

In this section, we saw where to locate the service worker in our browser. We then debugged it by unregistering it.

Summary

In this lesson, we worked entirely with service workers. We started by installing the required dependencies. We then moved on to enabling the service worker, configuring it, testing it, and finally, debugging it.

Index